WILLIAMS-SONOMA

COOKIES

RECIPES
MARIE SIMMONS

GENERAL EDITOR
CHUCK WILLIAMS

PHOTOGRAPHS
NOEL BARNHURST

SIMON & SCHUSTER • SOURCE

NEW YORK • LONDON • TORONTO • SYDNEY • SINGAPORE

CONTENTS

COOKIES FOR GIVING

HOLIDAY COOKIES

DECORATED COOKIES

INTRODUCTION

I have yet to meet anyone who can easily resist a home-baked cookie. And, because cookies are as easy and fun to make as they are to eat, you have every reason to try one of the tempting recipes in this book. Whether you prefer crisp cookies flavored with cinnamon and chopped nuts, dense chocolate bars with a touch of espresso, powdered sugar–dusted rounds filled with raspberry jam, or a buttery wedge of shortbread, you'll find more than a few favorites inside.

Each of these recipes is kitchen-tested to guarantee successful results and is accompanied by an informative side note that covers an essential ingredient or technique, helping you to make cookies that are always delicious. And, if you turn to the basics section in the back of the book, you will find additional tips, as well as creative ideas for packaging and presenting cookies as thoughtful gifts. I wish you much success with these recipes, which I hope you will share with all your family and friends.

Chuck Williams

THE CLASSICS

A freshly baked cookie, still warm from the oven, is perhaps the most beloved sweet treat. Here are all the popular favorites, from buttery shortbread and delicate madeleines to irresistible chocolate chip cookies and crunchy anise biscotti. Perfect for an afternoon pick-me-up or a late-night snack, these cookies can only be improved on by a cup of hot tea or a glass of cold milk.

CHOCOLATE CHIP COOKIES

Preheat the oven to 350°F (180°C). Have ready 2 ungreased baking sheets. Sift the flour, baking powder, baking soda, and salt onto a sheet of waxed paper; set aside.

In a large bowl, using an electric mixer on high speed, cream the butter until fluffy and pale yellow. Add the granulated and brown sugars and continue beating until the mixture is no longer gritty when rubbed between your finger and thumb. Add the egg and vanilla and beat on low speed until blended, occasionally stopping the mixer and scraping down the sides of the bowl with a rubber spatula as needed.

Add the flour mixture to the butter mixture and mix on low speed or stir with a wooden spoon just until blended. Add the chocolate chips and the walnuts, if using, mixing or stirring just until blended.

With dampened hands, shape the dough into 1-inch (2.5-cm) balls or drop by rounded tablespoons onto the baking sheets, spacing the cookies about 2 inches (5 cm) apart.

Bake the cookies until golden brown around the edges, about 12 minutes. Let the cookies cool briefly on the pans on wire racks before transferring them to the racks to cool completely.

MAKES ABOUT 4 DOZEN COOKIES

ABOUT CHIPS

To most people, the classic chocolate chip cookie is studded with semisweet (plain) chocolate chips, but your choice of chips is much greater. Markets now carry chips made of milk chocolate, white chocolate, peanut butter, and old-fashioned butterscotch. You can also choose between standard-sized chips, or morsels, and mini chips that are about half the size. Store chips of any flavor in an airtight container in a cool, dry place to avoid bloom, a harmless dusting of white that forms on the surface of chocolate when it has been exposed to extreme temperatures.

1⅓ cups (7 oz/220 g) all-purpose (plain) flour

½ teaspoon baking powder

½ teaspoon baking soda (bicarbonate of soda)

½ teaspoon salt

½ cup (4 oz/125 g) unsalted butter, at room temperature

½ cup (4 oz/125 g) granulated sugar

½ cup (3½ oz/105 g) firmly packed light brown sugar

1 large egg

1 teaspoon vanilla extract (essence)

1 cup (6 oz/185 g) semi-sweet (plain) chocolate chips

1 cup (4 oz/125 g) walnuts, toasted (page 22), then coarsely chopped (optional)

SCOTCH SHORTBREAD

1 cup (8 oz/250 g)
unsalted butter, at room
temperature

¼ cup (1 oz/30 g)
confectioners' (icing) sugar

¼ cup (2 oz/60 g)
granulated sugar, plus
1 tablespoon for sprinkling

2 teaspoons vanilla extract
(essence)

1½ cups (7½ oz/235 g)
all-purpose (plain) flour

¼ teaspoon salt

Preheat the oven to 300°F (150°C). Have ready an ungreased 9-inch (23-cm) square baking pan.

In a large bowl, using an electric mixer on high speed, cream the butter until fluffy and pale yellow. Add the confectioners' sugar and the ¼ cup granulated sugar and continue beating until the mixture is no longer gritty when rubbed between your finger and thumb. Beat in the vanilla.

Sift the flour and salt together onto a sheet of waxed paper. Gradually add the flour mixture to the butter mixture and mix on low speed or stir with a wooden spoon just until blended.

Using floured fingertips, press the dough evenly into the pan. Sprinkle evenly with the 1 tablespoon granulated sugar.

Bake the shortbread until the edges are golden, about 1 hour. Remove the pan from the oven and immediately use a thin, sharp knife to cut the shortbread into strips 3 inches by 1 inch (7.5 cm by 2.5 cm). Use a toothpick or the tines of a fork to decorate the shortbread with a pattern of dots. Let the strips cool in the pan on a wire rack for 30 minutes before transferring them to the rack to cool completely.

MAKES 27 BARS

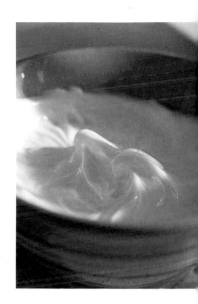

CREAMING BUTTER

A common first step in cookie recipes, creaming aerates the butter, resulting in cookies with a light, tender texture. To cream butter, beat it with an electric mixer or wooden spoon until it expands, lightens in color, and becomes soft and smooth. This should take 3–4 minutes by mixer, or longer by hand. Then add the sugar and beat until the grains are completely incorporated. Test by rubbing the mixture between your thumb and forefinger: It should feel smooth. Scrape down the sides of the bowl at least once during creaming to blend the ingredients evenly.

SUGAR COOKIES

In a large bowl, using an electric mixer on high speed, cream the butter until fluffy and pale. Add the granulated sugar in 3 additions, beating on low speed for 2 minutes after each addition. Beat the egg yolk and vanilla into the butter mixture until well blended.

Sift the flour and salt together onto a sheet of waxed paper. Add the flour mixture to the butter mixture and mix on low speed or stir with a wooden spoon just until blended.

Scrape the dough out onto a work surface and divide into 4 equal portions. Shape into disks, wrap in plastic wrap, and refrigerate for at least 2 hours or for up to overnight.

Preheat the oven to 350°F (180°C). Lightly grease 2 baking sheets or line them with parchment (baking) paper.

Remove the dough disks from the refrigerator and let stand at room temperature for about 15 minutes. Working with 1 disk at a time, roll out between 2 sheets of waxed paper to a thickness of ⅛–¼ inch (3–6 mm). Using cookie cutters, cut into circles or other shapes. Repeat with the remaining dough portions, then gather up the scraps and reroll them. If the scraps of dough have become sticky, refrigerate them for 10 minutes before rerolling. For best results, do not roll the same dough more than twice.

Using an offset spatula, transfer the cookies to the prepared pans. Sprinkle with sugar. (If using maple or confectioners' sugar, bake the cookies, then sprinkle with sugar while still warm.) If using an intricately shaped cutter, refrigerate the cutout cookies for 15–30 minutes before baking.

Bake the cookies until they are lightly golden on the bottom, 10–12 minutes. Let the cookies cool briefly on the pans on wire racks before transferring them to the racks to cool completely.

MAKES ABOUT 3 DOZEN COOKIES

FLAVOR VARIATIONS

For crisp sugar cookies with a smooth, dense chocolate taste, reduce the amount of flour in this recipe to 1¾ cups (9 oz/280 g) and add ½ cup (1½ oz/45 g) unsweetened Dutch-process cocoa powder. Sprinkle with granulated sugar or coarse sugar crystals, or decorate them with light-colored frosting, sprinkles, or shiny dragées. Or, after baking and cooling, dust the cookies generously with sifted confectioners' (icing) sugar. For a subtle citrus flavor, substitute 1 teaspoon lemon extract (essence) in place of the vanilla.

1¼ cups (12 oz/375 g) unsalted butter, at room temperature

¾ cup (6 oz/185 g) granulated sugar

1 large egg yolk

2 teaspoons vanilla extract (essence)

2 cups (10 oz/315 g) all-purpose (plain) flour

¼ teaspoon salt

Sugar for sprinkling, such as granulated, decorating, turbinado, maple, or confectioners' (icing)

LEMON BARS

FOR THE CRUST:

1 cup (5 oz/155 g)
all-purpose (plain) flour

¼ cup (1 oz/30 g)
confectioners' (icing) sugar

¼ teaspoon salt

1 teaspoon grated
lemon zest

½ cup (4 oz/125 g) cold
unsalted butter, cut into
small pieces

FOR THE FILLING:

3 tablespoons all-purpose
(plain) flour

½ cup (4 fl oz/125 ml)
fresh lemon juice

3 large eggs

1 cup (8 oz/250 g)
granulated sugar

1 tablespoon grated
lemon zest

Pinch of salt

Confectioners' (icing) sugar
for dusting

Preheat the oven to 350°F (180°C). Have ready a 13¾-by-4¼-inch (35-by-11-cm) oblong tart pan with a removable bottom, or an 8-inch (20-cm) square baking pan with bottom and sides lined with aluminum foil and generously greased.

To make the crust, sift the flour, confectioners' sugar, and salt together into a bowl and transfer to a food processor. Add the lemon zest and pulse to blend. Add the butter a few pieces at a time, processing just until the mixture is crumbly. Transfer the mixture to the prepared pan and press evenly into the bottom and sides to form the crust.

Bake until the crust is just golden at the edges, about 25 minutes.

Meanwhile, make the filling. In a large measuring cup or pitcher, whisk together the flour and lemon juice. Add the eggs, granulated sugar, lemon zest, and salt, and whisk until smooth. When the crust is baked, carefully pull out the oven rack and pour the filling into the crust. Close the oven door and reduce the heat to 325°F (165°C). Bake until the center is springy to the touch, about 30 minutes.

Transfer the pan to a wire rack and let cool completely. If using a tart pan with a removable bottom, place the pan on your out-stretched palm and let the rim fall away or, using the sides of the foil as handles, carefully lift the cookie from the pan and place it on a cutting board. Using a fine-mesh sieve, dust the cookie generously with confectioners' sugar (page 42). To make a striped pattern, lay strips of waxed paper across the cookie before dusting, and after dusting carefully remove the paper strips.

With a thin, sharp knife, cut crosswise into thin bars ¾–1 inch (2–2.5 cm wide) wide. Using a small, offset spatula, carefully remove the bars from the foil.

MAKES 12–16 BARS

ABOUT SIFTING

Sifting is a way of aerating a batter to make light, evenly textured cookies. It is also a way of combining dry ingredients to evenly distribute a leavener such as baking powder. If you don't have a sifter, simply pass the ingredients through a fine-mesh sieve. (For small amounts of flour, whisking produces the same effect.) Always follow a recipe exactly when it comes to sifting. Unless instructed otherwise, sift flour *after* measuring, since this will make a difference in the amount of flour used. See page 106 for general directions on measuring flour and other dry ingredients.

ANISE BISCOTTI

Preheat the oven to 350°F (180°C). Lightly grease and flour 1 large baking sheet, or line it with parchment (baking) paper, and have another ungreased baking sheet on hand.

In a large bowl, using an electric mixer on high speed, cream the butter until fluffy and pale yellow. Add the granulated sugar and continue beating until the mixture is no longer gritty when rubbed between your finger and thumb. Add the eggs one at a time, beating well on low speed after each addition. Beat in the vanilla, anise extract, and crushed aniseed on low speed until blended.

Sift the flour, baking powder, and salt together onto a sheet of waxed paper. Gradually add the flour mixture to the egg mixture and mix on low speed or stir with a wooden spoon just until blended. The batter should be very soft.

Turn the batter out onto a generously floured work surface and divide in half. With well-floured hands, transfer one-half onto the greased baking sheet and shape into a log about 12 inches (30 cm) long and 1½ inches (4 cm) in diameter. Place on one side of the sheet. Repeat with the remaining batter, leaving at least 4 inches (10 cm) between the logs. (They will spread as they bake.) Lightly brush the top of each log with some of the egg white and sprinkle with the coarse sugar crystals.

Bake the logs until the edges are golden, 25–30 minutes. Transfer the pan to a wire rack and let cool for 10 minutes. Using a serrated knife, cut the logs, still on the pan, on the diagonal into slices ½ inch (12 mm) wide. Carefully turn the slices on their sides and return them to the oven. When you run out of room on one baking sheet, start transferring slices to the other sheet. Bake until the edges are golden, about 10 minutes longer. Let cool completely on the pans on wire racks. Store in an airtight container.

MAKES ABOUT 4 DOZEN BISCOTTI

ANISEED

The seed of the anise plant, a member of the parsley family, aniseed is used whole or ground and has a sweet aroma and taste reminiscent of licorice. It is a popular addition to many European baked goods, as these typical Italian biscotti demonstrate. (For more information about biscotti, see page 67.) Aniseed is also one of the flavorings used in anisette, a popular European licorice-flavored liqueur.

½ cup (4 oz/125 g) unsalted butter, at room temperature

½ cup (4 oz/125 g) granulated sugar

2 large eggs

2 teaspoons vanilla extract (essence)

½ teaspoon anise extract (essence)

1 tablespoon aniseed, crushed

1¾ cups (9 oz/280 g) all-purpose (plain) flour

½ teaspoon baking powder

¼ teaspoon salt

1 egg white, lightly beaten

Coarse sugar crystals for sprinkling

MADELEINES

1¼ cups (5 oz/155 g) cake (soft-wheat) flour

¼ teaspoon baking powder

¼ teaspoon salt

2 large whole eggs plus 2 large egg yolks, at room temperature

¾ cup (6 oz/185 g) sugar

1 teaspoon vanilla extract (essence)

Grated zest of ½ lemon

½ cup (4 oz/125 g) unsalted butter, melted and cooled

Preheat the oven to 375°F (190°C). Generously brush a standard 12-mold madeleine pan with melted butter and lightly dust with flour, tapping out any excess. (If using a nonstick pan, there is no need to dust it with flour, but brushing with butter will add flavor.)

Sift the flour, baking powder, and salt together into a bowl. Set the dry ingredients aside.

In a large bowl, using an electric mixer on medium-high speed, beat the whole eggs, egg yolks, and sugar until light and fluffy. Add the vanilla and lemon zest and beat until combined.

Using a rubber spatula, fold the flour mixture into the egg mixture until blended. Add the melted butter and fold until well combined.

Drop the batter by heaping tablespoonfuls into the madeleine molds. Fill each mold three-fourths full. Bake until golden brown and springy to the touch, 15 minutes.

Immediately invert the pan onto a wire rack. If necessary, use a knife to pry the cookies gently from the pan. Let the cookies cool completely on the rack. Wipe out the pan, let cool, brush with melted butter, dust with flour, and repeat with the remaining batter.

MAKES 2 DOZEN MADELEINES

MADELEINES

French madeleines are delicate shell-shaped cookies with a light texture more like a sponge cake than a crisp, buttery cookie. Madeleines were made famous by Marcel Proust in his novel *Remembrance of Things Past* and have been a favorite accompaniment to tea and coffee ever since. Madeleines are baked in a traditional pan of the same name. Made of lightweight tinned steel, a standard madeleine pan has 12 molds.

LINZER COOKIES

TOASTING NUTS
To toast nuts, preheat the oven to 325°F (165°C). Spread the nuts in a single layer on a baking sheet, place in the oven and toast, stirring occasionally, until the nuts are fragrant and golden (or their papery skin starts to crack). Depending on the type and size of the nuts, this will take 10–20 minutes. Start checking after 10 minutes. Pour the nuts onto a plate to cool the moment they come out of the oven. They will continue to toast and may burn if left in the hot pan. To remove skins of nuts such as hazelnuts, rub them while still warm in a clean kitchen towel.

In a food processor, finely grind the toasted hazelnuts using short pulses (page 37). Set aside. In a large bowl, using an electric mixer on high speed, cream the butter until fluffy and pale yellow. Add the granulated sugar and continue beating until combined. Add the egg yolk, orange zest, vanilla, and almond extract and beat on low speed until blended.

Sift the flour, cinnamon, and salt together into another bowl. Add the ground hazelnuts and stir to blend. Add to the butter mixture and mix on low speed or stir with a wooden spoon until blended. The dough should be soft. Turn the dough out of the bowl, divide into 4 equal portions, and wrap each in plastic wrap. Refrigerate until chilled, about 1 hour.

Preheat the oven to 350°F (180°C). Lightly grease 2 baking sheets or line them with parchment (baking) paper. Remove 1 portion of the dough at a time from the refrigerator, place between 2 sheets of waxed paper, and roll out ¼ inch (6 mm) thick. Using a cookie cutter about 2½ inches (6 cm) in diameter, cut out the cookies. Cut a hole in the center of half of the cookies with a 1¼-inch (3-cm) cutter. Repeat to roll out all the dough, then reroll the dough scraps as needed to make 24 cutouts in all, cutting holes in half of them. If the dough becomes sticky, wrap it and chill in the freezer for 10 minutes before rolling out.

Using a thin spatula, carefully transfer the cookies to the prepared pans. Bake until firm to the touch, about 12 minutes. Transfer the pans to wire racks. Loosen the cookies from the pans with the spatula, but let remain in place until thoroughly cooled. To assemble, spread the solid cookies with a thin layer (about 1 teaspoon) of raspberry jam to within about ¼ inch (6 mm) of the edges. Dust the cutout cookies generously with confectioners' sugar (page 42). Top the solid cookies with the cutout cookies.

MAKES 12 COOKIES

1 cup (5 oz/155 g) hazelnuts (filberts) or slivered almonds, toasted and skinned *(far left)*

½ cup (4 oz/125 g) unsalted butter, at room temperature

½ cup (4 oz/125 g) granulated sugar

1 large egg yolk

1 teaspoon finely grated orange or lemon zest

¾ teaspoon vanilla extract (essence)

¼ teaspoon almond extract (essence)

1 cup (5 oz/155 g) all-purpose (plain) flour

½ teaspoon ground cinnamon

¼ teaspoon salt

About ¼ cup (2½ oz/75 g) seedless raspberry jam

Confectioners' (icing) sugar for dusting

COOKIES FOR KIDS

The fun shapes and bold flavors of these cookies appeal to young bakers and their grown-up helpers. Let younger kids try their hand at mixing chocolate chips into dough, while older kids can roll dough between their palms or layer sandwich cookies with sweet, creamy filling. The recipes in this chapter will become instant favorites with bakers of all ages.

OATMEAL COOKIES

In a saucepan over low heat, melt the butter, then remove from the heat. Using a wooden spoon, beat in the granulated and brown sugars until blended. Add the egg and vanilla and beat again until blended.

Sift the flour, baking soda, cinnamon, nutmeg, and salt together into a bowl. Stir the flour mixture into the egg mixture, then stir in the rolled oats and walnuts. Cover and refrigerate for 1 hour.

Preheat the oven to 350°F (180°C). Generously grease 2 baking sheets. Drop the batter by rounded tablespoons onto the prepared pans, spacing the cookies at least 2 inches (5 cm) apart. Using a metal spatula, flatten each mound of batter into a disk about ⅓ inch (9 mm) thick.

Bake the cookies until golden brown, 12–15 minutes. Transfer the cookies to wire racks to cool completely.

MAKES ABOUT 3 DOZEN COOKIES

Ingredients

½ cup (4 oz/125 g) unsalted butter

½ cup (4 oz/125 g) granulated sugar

½ cup (3½ oz/105 g) firmly packed dark brown sugar

1 large egg, lightly beaten

1 teaspoon vanilla extract (essence)

¾ cup (4 oz/125 g) all-purpose (plain) flour

¼ teaspoon baking soda (bicarbonate of soda)

¼ teaspoon ground cinnamon

¼ teaspoon ground nutmeg

¼ teaspoon salt

1½ cups (4½ oz/140 g) old-fashioned rolled oats

⅓ cup (1½ oz/45 g) finely chopped walnuts

DROP COOKIES

One of the simplest types of cookie to make is the drop cookie, so called because the batter is traditionally scooped up with a spoon and then "dropped" onto the baking sheet. To shape drop cookies, fill one spoon, usually a table-spoon, with batter, and then use a second spoon to push the batter off onto the baking sheet. If you prefer perfectly round cookies, roll the batter into balls between dampened palms. Be sure to space the cookies about 2 inches (5 cm) apart on the pans, as the batter is typically soft and buttery and the cookies will spread as they bake.

BROWNIES

½ cup (4 oz/125 g) unsalted butter, cut into 4 pieces

3 oz (90 g) unsweetened chocolate, finely chopped

1 cup (8 oz/250 g) sugar

Pinch of salt

2 large eggs, at room temperature

1 teaspoon vanilla extract (essence)

¾ cup (3 oz/90 g) cake (soft-wheat) flour, sifted

¾ cup (4½ oz/140 g) semisweet (plain) chocolate chips, peanut butter chips, or white chocolate chips (optional)

Preheat the oven to 350°F (180°C). Lightly grease an 8-inch (20-cm) square glass baking dish or metal pan.

In a saucepan over low heat, combine the butter and chopped unsweetened chocolate. Heat, stirring often, until melted, about 4 minutes. Remove from the heat and, using a wooden spoon, stir in the sugar and salt. Add the eggs and vanilla and stir until well blended. Sprinkle the sifted flour over the mixture and stir until just blended. Stir in the chips, if using.

Pour the batter into the prepared dish and spread evenly, smoothing the top. Bake the brownies until a toothpick inserted into the center comes out almost completely clean, about 30 minutes, or about 5 minutes longer if using a metal pan. Do not overbake. Transfer the pan to a wire rack to cool completely before cutting into 2½-inch (6-cm) squares.

MAKES 9 LARGE BARS

CHOCOLATE

The chocolate-making process begins with cocoa beans. The beans are fermented, roasted, shelled, and crushed into bits that are then ground and compressed to become chocolate liquor. Unsweetened, or bitter, chocolate is pure chocolate liquor with no sugar added. Depending on the amount of sugar added, the chocolate liquor becomes the more familiar semisweet and sweet chocolate. The addition of milk solids results in milk chocolate. Always use the chocolate type specified in the recipe, as different varieties behave differently and should not be substituted.

BLONDIES

Preheat the oven to 350°F (180°C). Grease an 8-inch (20-cm) square baking pan, line the bottom with parchment (baking) paper, and grease the parchment.

Sift the flour and salt together onto a sheet of waxed paper, and set aside.

In a saucepan over medium heat, combine the butter and brown sugar. Heat, stirring often, until the sugar has dissolved. Continue to cook about 1 minute longer; the mixture will bubble but not boil. Set aside to cool, about 10 minutes.

Add the egg, egg yolk, and vanilla to the cooled sugar mixture and stir with a wooden spoon to combine. Sprinkle the sifted flour and salt over the sugar mixture and stir until just blended.

Pour the batter into the prepared pan, spreading it evenly with a spatula and smoothing the top. Bake until the center is springy to the touch and a toothpick inserted into the center comes out clean, 25–35 minutes. Do not overbake. Transfer the pan to a wire rack until cool enough to handle.

Run a small knife around the inside of the pan to loosen the cookie. Invert onto the rack, lift off the pan, and then carefully peel off the parchment paper. Let cool completely on the rack before cutting into 2-inch (5-cm) squares.

MAKES 16 BARS

1 cup (5 oz/155 g) plus
2 tablespoons all-purpose
(plain) flour

¼ teaspoon salt

½ cup (4 oz/125 g)
unsalted butter

1½ cups (10½ oz/330 g)
firmly packed light brown
sugar

1 large egg plus 1 large
egg yolk, at room
temperature

1½ teaspoons vanilla
extract (essence)

CHOCOLATE COOKIE SANDWICHES

¾ cup (6 oz/185 g) unsalted butter, at room temperature

¾ cup (6 oz/185 g) granulated sugar

2 large eggs

1 teaspoon vanilla extract (essence)

½ cup (2½ oz/75 g) all-purpose (plain) flour

½ cup (1½ oz/45 g) unsweetened Dutch-process cocoa powder

¼ teaspoon baking powder

¼ teaspoon baking soda (bicarbonate of soda)

⅛ teaspoon salt

PEANUT BUTTER FILLING:

4 tablespoons (2 oz/60 g) unsalted butter, at room temperature

½ cup (2 oz/60 g) confectioners' (icing) sugar

½ cup (5 oz/155 g) creamy peanut butter

½ teaspoon vanilla extract (essence)

In a large bowl, using an electric mixer on high speed or a wooden spoon, cream the butter until fluffy and pale yellow. Add the granulated sugar and continue beating until the mixture is no longer gritty when rubbed between your finger and thumb. Add the eggs and vanilla and stir or beat on low speed until blended.

Sift the flour, cocoa, baking powder, baking soda, and salt together onto a sheet of waxed paper. Add to the butter mixture and beat or stir just until blended. Cover and refrigerate the dough until firm, about 2 hours.

Preheat the oven to 350°F (180°C). Lightly grease 2 baking sheets.

With dampened hands, shape the dough into ¾-inch (2-cm) balls, and place 2 inches (5 cm) apart on the prepared baking sheets. Using a spatula or the bottom of a glass that has been dusted with cocoa to prevent sticking, press down on each dough ball to flatten slightly. Bake the cookies until firm to the touch, 10–12 minutes. Transfer the cookies to wire racks to cool completely.

Meanwhile, make the peanut butter filling. Combine the butter, confectioners' sugar, peanut butter, and vanilla extract in a large bowl. Beat with a wooden spoon until blended and smooth. Cover and refrigerate until the cookies are cool.

Spread the flat side of half the cookies with 1½ teaspoons of the peanut butter filling. Top each with a second cookie, flat side down. Press lightly to make a cookie sandwich.

Storage Tip: Store these cookies tightly covered in a cool place, or refrigerate in warm weather.

MAKES ABOUT 3 DOZEN FILLED COOKIES

PEANUT BUTTER
Made by grinding dry-roasted peanuts to a paste, peanut butter is a favorite food of young and old alike. It is available in two styles, creamy, or smooth, and chunky, that is, with finely chopped nuts mixed in for texture. Natural peanut butters are made without the additives that ease spreadability. They have a somewhat grainy consistency and a layer of oil on top that must be stirred in before using.

BLACK-AND-WHITE COOKIES

Lightly grease 2 baking sheets or line with parchment (baking) paper. Set aside.

In a food processor, combine the flour, sugar, and salt. Add the butter pieces in 2 additions, pulsing after each addition, until the mixture has the consistency of coarse crumbs. Add the egg yolk and vanilla and pulse until the dough holds together.

Divide the dough in half. Transfer one-half to a lightly floured work surface and knead in the cocoa until incorporated.

Lightly dust the work surface and a rolling pin with flour. Roll out each dough half into a 3-by-9-inch (7.5-by-23-cm) rectangle, ½–¾ inch (12 mm–2 cm) thick; trim the edges to even out. Place each rectangle on a large baking sheet and cover with plastic wrap. Refrigerate until well chilled, about 30 minutes. Meanwhile, in a small bowl, beat the whole egg until blended. Set aside.

Remove the dough from the refrigerator. Using a sharp knife, cut each rectangle into 4 strips about ¾ inches (2 cm) wide (you should have 4 strips of each color). Arrange 2 chocolate strips and 2 plain strips in a checkerboard pattern, brushing the beaten egg between the strips and gently pressing together. Repeat with the remaining dough. Wrap in plastic and use a knife to square off the edges of each block. Refrigerate until well chilled, about 30 minutes. Preheat the oven to 350°F (180°C).

Remove the blocks from the refrigerator, unwrap, and cut each crosswise into slices ¼ inch (6 mm) thick. Place 1½ inches (4 cm) apart on the prepared sheets and bake until they feel firm when lightly pressed, about 15 minutes. Let the cookies sit on the baking sheets for 2 minutes before using a spatula to transfer them to wire racks to cool completely.

MAKES ABOUT 5 DOZEN COOKIES

2 cups (10 oz/315 g) all-purpose (plain) flour

½ cup (4 oz/125 g) sugar

Pinch of salt

1 cup (8 oz/250 g) cold unsalted butter, cut into small pieces

1 large whole egg plus 1 large egg yolk

½ teaspoon vanilla extract (essence)

3 tablespoons unsweetened Dutch-process cocoa powder

ICEBOX COOKIES

Also known as refrigerator cookies, icebox cookies are made by forming dough into a log or rectangular block and chilling it thoroughly. You can also use different types of dough together—vanilla and chocolate, peanut butter and chocolate—to make patterned cookies. Cookies are then sliced off the log or block and baked. When slicing the dough, give the block or log a quarter turn after every half dozen or so slices to keep the cookies perfectly square or round.

NUTTY BUTTER BALLS

2 cups (8 oz/250 g) pecans

1 cup (8 oz/250 g) unsalted butter, at room temperature

¾ cup (6 oz/185 g) firmly packed light brown sugar

1 large egg, separated

1½ teaspoons vanilla extract (essence)

2 cups (10 oz/315 g) all-purpose (plain) flour

½ teaspoon salt

¼ teaspoon baking powder

½ cup (4 oz/125 g) multicolored coarse sugar crystals

In a food processor, finely grind the pecans (*right*). Measure out ¾ cup (3 oz/90 g) for the batter. Reserve the remaining ground nuts for coating the cookies. Set aside.

In a large bowl, using an electric mixer on high speed or a wooden spoon, cream the butter until fluffy and pale yellow. Add the brown sugar and continue beating until the mixture is no longer gritty when rubbed between your finger and thumb. Add the egg yolk and vanilla and beat on low speed or stir until blended.

Sift the flour, salt, and baking powder together onto a sheet of waxed paper. Gradually add the flour mixture to the butter mixture, mixing on low speed or stirring with a wooden spoon until blended. Mix or stir in the ¾ cup (3 oz/90 g) ground pecans just until blended.

Preheat the oven to 350°F (180°C). Have ready 2 baking sheets. Lightly grease the pans or line them with parchment (baking) paper, or alternatively have ready about 4 dozen miniature paper muffin liners. Spread the remaining ground pecans in a shallow bowl. Lightly beat the egg white in a small bowl.

With floured hands, shape the dough into ¾-inch (2-cm) balls. Brush the balls lightly with egg white and roll in the pecans to coat lightly. Place each ball in a paper liner, if using. Place the cookies about 1 inch (2.5 cm) apart on the prepared pans. Pour the sugar crystals into a shallow bowl and reserve.

Bake until the bottoms are lightly browned, 15–18 minutes. Let cool slightly on the pans on wire racks. Using a wide, flexible metal spatula, remove the warm cookies from the baking sheets and roll them in the sugar crystals to coat, or sprinkle the sugar on top if in paper liners. Let cool completely on wire racks.

MAKES ABOUT 5 DOZEN COOKIES

GRINDING NUTS

To grind nuts, use a hand-cranked nut grinder or process in a food processor using short pulses to yield a coarse, crumbly texture. If using a food processor, beware of overprocessing the nuts into a smooth paste, which releases their oils and diminishes their flavor. For best results, combine the nuts with a little of the flour or sugar called for in the recipe and process for no longer than 5 to 10 seconds at a time.

CRISP CHOCOLATE BITES

COCOA POWDER

This rich velvety powder is made by removing nearly all of the cocoa butter from chocolate liquor and then grinding it to an unsweetened powder. Do not confuse cocoa powder with sweetened cocoa mixes. Dutch-processed, or alkalized, cocoa is treated with an alkali to make it less sharp in flavor than nonalkalized cocoa powder. Either will work in this recipe.

Lightly grease 2 baking sheets or line with parchment (baking) paper. Set aside.

In a small saucepan over very low heat, combine the butter and chocolate. Cook, stirring occasionally, just until they are melted and the mixture is smooth.

Pour the chocolate mixture into a large bowl and let cool slightly. Stir in the granulated sugar until evenly moistened. Add the egg and vanilla, beating until light and fluffy.

Sift the flour, cocoa, baking soda, and salt together onto a sheet of waxed paper. Gradually add the flour mixture to the chocolate mixture and stir to combine. Cover and refrigerate until firm, about 1 hour.

Preheat the oven to 375°F (190°C). Remove the cookie dough from the refrigerator. Shape the dough into ¾-inch (2-cm) balls and roll in the confectioners' sugar to coat completely. Place the balls about 1½ inches (4 cm) apart on the prepared sheets. Bake the cookies until puffed and cracked on top, about 12 minutes. They may appear underdone in the center but will turn crisp as they cool. Let cool on the sheets for 2–3 minutes, then transfer the cookies to a wire rack to cool completely.

MAKES ABOUT 3½ DOZEN COOKIES

6 tablespoons (3 oz/90 g) unsalted butter, cut into pieces

2 oz (60 g) unsweetened chocolate, chopped

1 cup (8 oz/250 g) granulated sugar

1 large egg

1 teaspoon vanilla extract (essence)

¾ cup (4 oz/125 g) all-purpose (plain) flour

¼ cup (¾ oz/20 g) unsweetened Dutch-process cocoa powder

½ teaspoon baking soda (bicarbonate of soda)

¼ teaspoon salt

½ cup (2 oz/60 g) confectioners' (icing) sugar

PARTY COOKIES

Tempting and sweet, cookies are the perfect party food. In this chapter, you'll find recipes to suit every occasion, from a bridal shower to a Christmas Eve get-together. Add an elegant touch to any dessert table with sugar-dusted raspberry gems or almond-flecked tuiles. Each of the festive treats below also is easy to prepare and makes a beautiful presentation.

RUBY JEWEL COOKIES

Preheat the oven to 350°F (180°C). Have ready 2 ungreased baking sheets or miniature muffin pans and, if desired, about 5 dozen miniature paper muffin liners.

In a small bowl, whisk the egg yolks and vanilla together; set aside.

Combine the flour and granulated sugar in a food processor and process just to blend. With the machine running, add the butter 2 or 3 pieces at a time and process until the mixture looks crumbly. With the machine still running, add the egg yolk mixture and process until blended and the dough begins to pull away from the sides of the bowl.

Turn the dough out onto a sheet of plastic wrap and shape it into a flat disk. Wrap and refrigerate until chilled, about 1 hour.

With lightly floured hands, shape the dough into ¾-inch (2-cm) balls. Place each ball in a paper liner, if using. Place the cookies 1 inch (2.5 cm) apart on the baking sheets or in the muffin pans.

Using the end of a wooden spoon handle dipped in flour to prevent sticking, make an indentation in the center of each cookie, but do not press all the way through the dough. Using a spoon or a pastry bag fitted with a plain tip (page 53), fill each indentation with about ¼ teaspoon jam.

Bake the cookies until the edges are golden, 15–20 minutes. Let the cookies cool completely on the pans on wire racks. (If baking on sheets without paper liners, use a thin spatula to loosen the cookies carefully while they are still warm.) Transfer the cooled cookies to wire racks and, using a fine-mesh sieve, dust with confectioners' sugar.

MAKES ABOUT 5 DOZEN COOKIES

DUSTING WITH SUGAR

Sifting delicate confectioners' sugar over cookies adds a pretty finishing touch. Confectioners' sugar, also called powdered sugar or icing sugar, is granulated sugar that has been finely crushed and mixed with a little cornstarch (cornflour). Always sift confectioners' sugar before adding to cookie dough or using for decorating, as it has a tendency to form tiny lumps. To dust cookies, put the sugar in a fine-mesh sieve and tap the sieve gently as you move it over the cookies.

2 large egg yolks

1 teaspoon vanilla extract (essence)

2¼ cups (11½ oz/360 g) all-purpose (plain) flour

⅔ cup (5 oz/155 g) granulated sugar

1 cup (8 oz/250 g) cold unsalted butter, cut into small pieces

About ⅓ cup (3½ oz/ 105 g) seedless raspberry jam or other thick jam

Confectioners' (icing) sugar for dusting

ALMOND SAND COOKIES

⅔ cup (5 oz/155 g) sugar

½ cup (2½ oz/75 g) chopped blanched almonds, plus ¾ cup (4 oz/125 g) whole almonds

¾ cup (6 fl oz/180 ml) browned butter *(far right)*, cooled slightly

¼ teaspoon almond extract (essence)

1¾ cups (9 oz/280 g) all-purpose (plain) flour

2 teaspoons baking powder

Pinch of salt

1 large egg white, lightly beaten

In a food processor, combine the sugar and chopped almonds and finely grind using short pulses (page 37).

Combine the browned butter and almond mixture in a large bowl. Stir with a wooden spoon until evenly moistened. Stir in the almond extract.

Sift the flour, baking powder, and salt together onto a sheet of waxed paper. Stir the flour mixture into the butter mixture just until blended.

Preheat the oven to 300°F (150°C). Lightly grease 2 baking sheets or line them with parchment (baking) paper.

With lightly floured hands, shape the dough into ¾-inch (2-cm) balls. Place 1 inch (2.5 cm) apart on the prepared baking sheets. Lightly brush the top of each ball with beaten egg white and press a whole almond down into the center. Pinch together any cracks that appear around the edges of the cookies.

Bake the cookies until golden, about 20 minutes. Let the cookies cool completely on the pans on wire racks before carefully removing them with a thin spatula.

Make-Ahead Tip: These cookies benefit from being made ahead of time, as their flavor improves after 2 or 3 days. Store the cookies between layers of waxed paper in an airtight container for up to 1 week.

MAKES ABOUT 3½ DOZEN COOKIES

BROWNED BUTTER

Browned butter adds a deep flavor to these cookies. To brown the butter, melt 1 cup (8 oz/250 g) unsalted butter, cut into chunks, in a frying pan over medium heat until it foams. Reduce the heat to low and cook until the foam along the edges begins to turn golden, about 5 minutes. Remove from the heat and pour into a heatproof measuring pitcher or bowl. Let stand for 5 minutes. Spoon off the foam that rises to the top, and pour the clear liquid into a clean vessel, leaving the browned bits behind. You should have about ¾ cup (6 fl oz/180 ml).

NEAPOLITAN COOKIES

In a large bowl, using an electric mixer on high speed, cream the butter until it is fluffy and pale yellow. Add the sugar and continue beating until the mixture is no longer gritty. Beat in the egg, vanilla, and salt on low speed until well blended. Sift the flour and baking powder together onto a sheet of waxed paper and gradually beat or stir into the butter mixture just until blended.

Divide the dough evenly among 3 bowls. Stir and knead the chocolate and pecans into the first bowl, the food coloring into the second bowl, and the nutmeg into the third bowl.

Line a 9-by-5-inch (23-by-13-cm) loaf pan with a sheet of waxed paper, overlapping the long sides by about 3 inches (7.5 cm). Scrape the nutmeg batter into the pan and, with a small offset spatula, press to the edges in an even layer. Smooth out the dough with your fingertips. Drop the pink-tinted batter by teaspoons onto the nutmeg layer and press into an even layer. Smooth with your fingertips. Repeat with the chocolate batter. Fold the waxed paper over the top and press to smooth and compress the layers. Refrigerate until firm, at least 24 hours or up to 2 days.

Preheat the oven to 350°F (180°C). Lightly butter 2 baking sheets or line them with parchment (baking) paper. Use the paper to lift the dough out of the pan. Invert onto a wooden board and remove the paper. Using a long, thin knife, cut it in half lengthwise. Cut crosswise into slices ¼ inch (6 mm) thick to make striped cookies.

Transfer the slices to the prepared sheets, placing the cookies at least 1½ inches (4 cm) apart. Bake the cookies until set and pale gold on the bottom, about 15 minutes. Let the cookies cool on the sheets on wire racks for a few minutes before transferring them to the racks to cool completely.

MAKES ABOUT 6 DOZEN COOKIES

NUTMEG

The oval, brown seed of a soft fruit, nutmeg has a warm, sweet, spicy flavor. Inside the fruit, the nutmeg seed is enclosed in a lacy red cage that, when lifted away and ground, is known as the spice mace. In small amounts, nutmeg acts as a subtle flavor booster in savory dishes, but it is most frequently used to flavor sweet treats, from custards to cakes to cookies. Whole nutmeg keeps its flavor much longer than ground nutmeg. Always grate nutmeg just before using. Use the finest rasps on a box grater-shredder, or a specialized nutmeg grater.

1 cup (8 oz/250 g) unsalted butter, at room temperature

1¼ cups (10 oz/315 g) sugar

1 large egg

1 teaspoon vanilla extract (essence)

¼ teaspoon salt

2¼ cups (11½ oz/360 g) all-purpose (plain) flour

1¼ teaspoons baking powder

1 oz (30 g) unsweetened chocolate, chopped, melted, and slightly cooled (page 50)

¼ cup (1 oz/30 g) finely chopped pecans

1 or 2 drops red food coloring

¼ teaspoon freshly grated nutmeg

CHOCOLATE ESPRESSO BARS

¾ cup (4 oz/125 g) all-purpose (plain) flour

½ cup (1½ oz/45 g) unsweetened Dutch-process cocoa powder

3 tablespoons instant espresso powder

¼ teaspoon baking powder

¼ teaspoon salt

½ cup (4 oz/125 g) unsalted butter, cut into pieces

2 oz (60 g) semisweet (plain) chocolate, coarsely chopped

2 large eggs

1 cup (7 oz/220 g) firmly packed light brown sugar

1 teaspoon vanilla extract (essence)

FOR THE GLAZE:

¼ cup (2 fl oz/60 ml) heavy (double) cream

1 teaspoon instant espresso powder

4 oz (125 g) semisweet (plain) chocolate, chopped

Pinch of salt

16 chocolate-covered espresso beans (optional)

Preheat the oven to 350°F (180°C). Generously grease an 8-inch (20-cm) square baking pan.

Sift the flour, cocoa powder, espresso powder, baking powder, and salt together into a bowl; set aside.

Combine the butter and chocolate in a small, heavy saucepan and place over low heat, stirring occasionally, until melted, about 2 minutes. Remove from the heat and let cool slightly.

In a bowl, whisk the eggs and brown sugar together until blended. Gradually stir in the melted chocolate mixture until blended. Stir in the vanilla, then add the flour mixture and stir until blended.

Pour the batter into the prepared pan. Bake until the edges pull away from the sides of the pan and the center is springy to the touch, about 25 minutes. Let cool in the pan on a wire rack.

Meanwhile, make the glaze. In a small saucepan over medium heat, combine the heavy cream and espresso powder and heat, stirring, just until the powder is dissolved and bubbles start to appear around the pan edges. Add the chocolate and salt, remove from the heat, and stir just until the chocolate is melted. Let cool to room temperature.

Using a small offset spatula, spread the cooled glaze over the cookie in a thin layer. Refrigerate until the glaze is set, about 30 minutes. Cut into 1½-by-2½-inch (4-by-6-cm) bars or 2-inch (5-cm) squares. If desired, top each bar with a chocolate-covered espresso bean.

MAKES 16 BARS

ESPRESSO

Instant espresso powder offers the most practical way to impart a good, rich coffee flavor to cookies, candies, and cakes. Sold in well-stocked food markets and specialty coffee stores, the fine powder dissolves quickly in hot liquid, to produce a bolder, more concentrated taste than regular instant coffee. This intense flavor comes with a solid dose of caffeine, however, so if you are sensitive to caffeine's effects, look for a brand of instant espresso powder labeled "decaffeinated."

ALMOND CRISPS DRIZZLED WITH CHOCOLATE

MELTING CHOCOLATE

To melt chocolate without burning, use a double boiler, which consists of two nesting saucepans and is used for gentle heating. Pour water into the bottom pan, keeping it shallow enough that it does not touch the top pan. Heat the water to a gentle simmer and place the chocolate in the top pan. Adjust the heat to keep the water at a bare simmer. Any contact with moisture can cause chocolate to seize, or stiffen, so make sure the fit between the pans is snug and no steam escapes. (If you do not have a double boiler, assemble one using a saucepan and a heatproof bowl that rests tightly on top.)

In a large bowl, using an electric mixer on high speed, cream the butter until it is fluffy and pale yellow. Add the brown sugar and continue to beat on high speed until the mixture is no longer gritty when rubbed between your finger and thumb. Add the egg and vanilla and beat on low speed until blended.

Sift the flour, baking powder, and salt together onto a sheet of waxed paper. Add to the butter mixture and mix on low speed or stir with a wooden spoon until well blended. Stir in the almonds.

Preheat the oven to 400°F (200°C). Have ready 2 ungreased, preferably nonstick, baking sheets.

Drop the batter by level teaspoons onto the baking sheets, spacing the cookies at least 2 inches (5 cm) apart. Bake until the edges turn golden but the cookies are still soft, about 5 minutes. Let the cookies cool on the pans on wire racks for exactly 5 minutes before carefully transferring them to the racks to cool completely.

To make the chocolate glaze, put the chocolate and the shortening, if using, in the top of a double boiler over barely simmering water *(left)* and stir until melted and blended. Alternatively, combine in a glass bowl and microwave on high for 1 minute, or until shiny and soft. Stir to even out the texture.

Using the tines of a fork, drizzle the chocolate on the top of a cooled cookie. Repeat with the remaining cookies. Set on wire racks and let cool until set, about 1 hour. To hasten cooling, refrigerate the cookies for about 15 minutes.

Note: If you want the chocolate glaze to remain shiny after it cools, add the shortening, which will also prevent the glaze from cracking.

MAKES ABOUT 6 DOZEN COOKIES

½ cup (4 oz/125 g) unsalted butter, at room temperature

1 cup (7 oz/220 g) firmly packed light brown sugar

1 large egg

1 teaspoon vanilla extract (essence)

¾ cup (4 oz/125 g) all-purpose (plain) flour

1 teaspoon baking powder

½ teaspoon salt

½ cup (2 oz/60 g) finely chopped almonds

FOR THE CHOCOLATE GLAZE:

6 oz (185 g) semisweet (plain) chocolate, chopped

1 teaspoon solid vegetable shortening (vegetable lard) (optional; see Note)

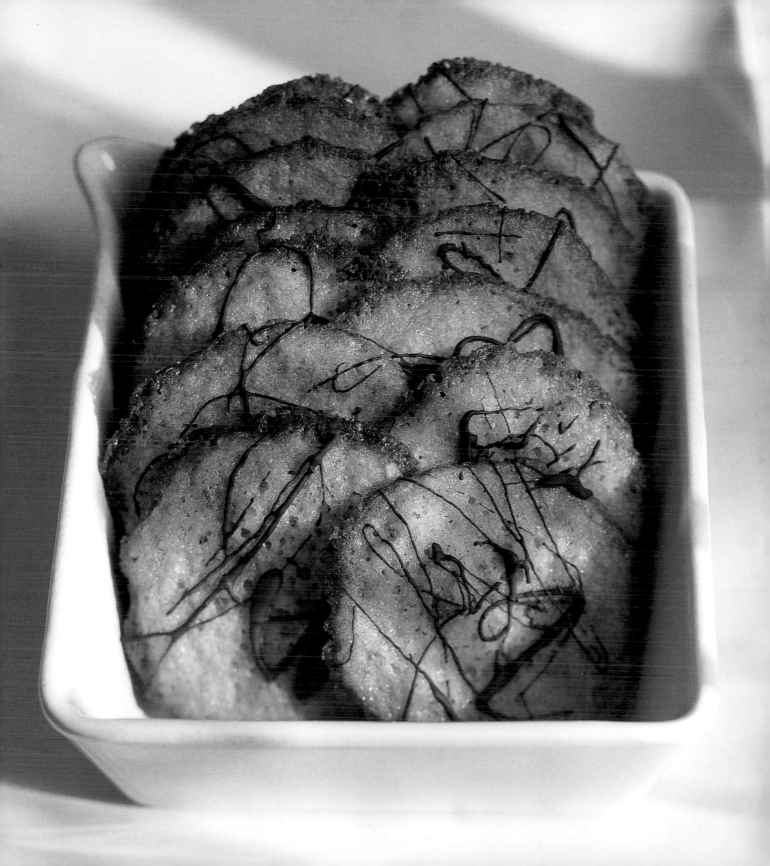

PEANUT BUTTER COOKIES

½ cup (4 oz/125 g) unsalted butter, melted

½ cup (3½ oz/105 g) firmly packed light brown sugar

½ cup (4 oz/125 g) granulated sugar

1 cup (10 oz/315 g) creamy peanut butter

1 large egg

1 teaspoon vanilla extract (essence)

1⅓ cups (7 oz/220 g) all-purpose (plain) flour

½ teaspoon baking powder

½ teaspoon baking soda (bicarbonate of soda)

½ teaspoon salt

3 oz (90 g) semisweet (plain) chocolate, melted (optional; page 50)

In a large bowl, using an electric mixture on medium speed or a wooden spoon, beat the melted butter, brown and granulated sugars, peanut butter, egg, and vanilla until well blended.

Sift the flour, baking powder, baking soda, and salt together onto a sheet of waxed paper. Add the flour mixture to the butter mixture and mix on low speed or stir with the wooden spoon just until combined. Cover and refrigerate until firm, about 2 hours.

Preheat the oven to 350°F (180°C). Generously grease 2 baking sheets. Using dampened hands, shape the dough into 1-inch (2.5 cm) balls. Place 2 inches (5 cm) apart on the prepared baking sheets. Using the tines of a fork dipped in flour, lightly press on each dough ball to flatten slightly and make a pattern of parallel indentations.

Bake until the bottoms are golden brown, 12–15 minutes. Let the cookies cool briefly on the pans. Using a wide, flexible metal spatula, transfer the warm cookies to the racks to cool completely.

If desired, use a pastry bag fitted with a narrow tip to pipe melted chocolate into the grooves of each cookie (right).

MAKES ABOUT 3 DOZEN COOKIES

PASTRY BAG BASICS
To give these cookies a decorative touch, pipe melted chocolate into the indentations made by the fork tines: Fit a pastry, or piping, bag, with a very small plain tip. Fold down the edge of the bag, creating a cuff, and fill the bag no more than halfway full with the chocolate. Unfold the top and twist it to squeeze the chocolate firmly toward the tip. Holding the bag at a 45-degree angle with one hand, and maintaining a small gap between the tip and the cookie, squeeze the bag to release the chocolate in an even line.

BROWN SUGAR TUILES

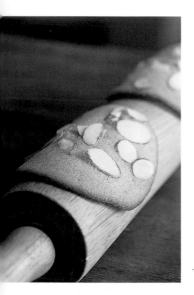

Preheat the oven to 350°F (180°C). Line a baking sheet with parchment (baking) paper.

Combine the egg whites, brown sugar, vanilla, and salt in a large bowl and whisk until smooth. Add the butter and flour and stir until blended.

Using 1 tablespoon of the batter for each cookie, spread 4-inch (10-cm) circles on the prepared baking sheets with an icing spatula or small offset spatula. Sprinkle each cookie with about 1 teaspoon of the nuts, if using. Do not make more than 5 cookies at a time.

Bake the cookies until the edges are browned and center is golden, 6–8 minutes. Remove the baking sheet from the oven. Working quickly while the cookies are very hot, carefully lift them from the baking sheet with a wide spatula. Drape the cookies over a rolling pin or other long, smooth cylinder. Let cool for about 1 minute. The cookies will firm up quickly but are still rather fragile. Carefully transfer them to a wire rack and let cool completely.

Form and bake the remaining cookies in batches, working with just 4 or 5 cookies at a time. Let cool completely.

Serving Tip: For an elegant dessert, serve these cookies alongside a scoop of vanilla ice cream.

MAKES ABOUT 20 COOKIES

ABOUT TUILES

Tuile means "tile" in French, and these delicate cookies are named for the curved terra-cotta tiles traditionally found on roofs in the Mediterranean.

They are made by dropping batter onto a baking sheet and then spreading it into large, thin, even circles. Always bake tuiles in small batches, and be ready to shape them as soon as they come out of the oven: Using a wide, flexible metal spatula, lift each hot cookie from the pan and drape it over a rolling pin, a narrow bottle, or a similar object. As soon as the cookies are set, after no more than 1 minute, carefully transfer to a wire rack to cool.

2 large egg whites

½ cup (3½ oz/105 g) firmly packed light brown sugar

1 teaspoon vanilla extract (essence)

Pinch of salt

6 tablespoons (3 oz/90 g) unsalted butter, melted and cooled

½ cup (2½ oz/75 g) all-purpose (plain) flour

½ cup (2 oz/60 g) sliced almonds or finely chopped pistachios (optional)

CIGARETTES RUSSES

6 tablespoons (3 oz/90 g) unsalted butter, at room temperature

1 cup (4 oz/125 g) confectioners' (icing) sugar

4 large egg whites, at room temperature

2 teaspoons vanilla extract (essence)

⅔ cup (3 oz/90 g) all-purpose (plain) flour

⅛ teaspoon salt

FOR THE CHOCOLATE DIP:

3 oz (90 g) semisweet (plain) chocolate, chopped

1½ teaspoons unsalted butter

1 teaspoon light corn syrup

Preheat the oven to 425°F (220°C). Grease 2 large baking sheets or line with silicone liners *(right)*.

In a large bowl, using an an electric mixer on high speed, cream the butter until fluffy and pale yellow. Gradually add the confectioners' sugar and continue beating until well blended. Add the egg whites, one-fourth at a time, beating well after each addition. Add the vanilla and beat until blended.

Sift the flour and salt together onto a sheet of waxed paper. Gradually stir the flour mixture into the butter mixture.

Drop the batter by level tablespoonfuls onto a prepared sheet, spacing them about 5 inches (13 cm) apart and forming only 4 cookies. (The cookies must be baked in small batches, because, once baked, they must be shaped quickly before they cool.) Using a lightly moistened offset spatula or the back of a spoon, spread the batter into thin ovals about 3 by 4 inches (7.5 by 10 cm).

Bake the cookies until they are just golden at the edges, about 3 minutes. Meanwhile, prepare a second batch on the remaining sheet. Remove the baked cookies from the oven. Working quickly, use a thin, flexible metal spatula to remove 1 baked cookie at a time and wrap it lengthwise around the handle of a wooden spoon to make a hollow tube. Transfer to a wire rack to cool and repeat with the remaining 3 cookies. If the cookies become too cool to shape easily, return them to the oven for 30 seconds to soften. Continue baking and rolling the remaining batter.

To make the chocolate dip, combine the chocolate, butter, and corn syrup in the top of a double boiler over barely simmering water (page 50); stir until melted and blended. Let cool slightly. Dip about 1 inch (2.5 cm) of each cookie into the chocolate. Place on a wire rack, with the dipped end not touching the rack, until set.

MAKES ABOUT 3 DOZEN COOKIES

SILICONE LINERS

Silicone-coated fiberglass baking mats are reusable nonstick liners that may be used any time a recipe calls for a greased or lined pan. They are especially handy for these very thin, delicate cookies, which are made from a liquidy batter that spreads on the baking sheet. The liners also promote uniform browning. They come in a range of sizes and can withstand oven temperatures of up to 500°F (260°C). To clean the mats, just wipe them with a soft, clean cloth.

COOKIES FOR GIVING

Home-baked cookies are a warm and thoughtful gift for any occasion. The cookies in this chapter use ingredients such as oatmeal, molasses, dried fruits, nuts, and spices, which means they can be made in advance and will still taste wonderful. Some will improve with time, as the spices and other flavorings marry. And all are ideal for giving or sending to family and friends.

PISTACHIO-SPICE COOKIES

In a large bowl, using an electric mixer on high speed, cream the butter until fluffy and pale yellow. Add the brown sugar and continue beating until the mixture is no longer gritty when rubbed between your finger and thumb. Add the molasses, egg yolks, and almond extract; beat on medium speed or stir with a wooden spoon just until blended.

Sift the flour, cinnamon, cardamom, baking soda, and salt together onto a sheet of waxed paper. Add the flour mixture to the butter mixture in 4 additions, mixing on low speed or stirring until blended after each addition. Mix or stir in the pistachios until evenly distributed. The dough will appear dry and crumbly.

Turn the dough out onto a lightly floured work surface and press it into a round, smooth disk. Divide the dough in half, and roll each half into a log about 6 inches (15 cm) long. Flatten and square off each log, making a rectangular shape about 6 inches (15 cm) long, 3 inches (7.5 cm) wide, and 1½ inches (4 cm) thick. Wrap each rectangle in plastic wrap and refrigerate for at least 2 hours or preferably for 24 hours.

When ready to bake, preheat the oven to 325°F (165°C). Lightly grease 2 baking sheets or line them with parchment (baking) paper.

Using a sharp, thin knife, cut the chilled dough into slices ⅛ inch (3 mm) thick. Transfer the slices to the prepared pans, placing them 1 inch (2.5 cm) apart. Bake the cookies until the edges are golden, 10–12 minutes. Let the cookies cool on the pans on wire racks for 2 minutes before transferring them to the racks to cool completely.

MAKES ABOUT 4 DOZEN COOKIES

SEPARATING EGGS

Eggs are easier to separate when they are cold. Carefully crack each egg and, holding it over a bowl, pass the yolk back and forth between the shell halves, letting the whites fall into the bowl. Drop the yolk into a separate bowl, and transfer the whites to a third bowl. Separate each additional egg over the empty bowl, for if any speck of yolk gets into the whites, the whites will not whip up properly. If a yolk breaks, start fresh with a new egg. Egg whites will keep for up to 5 days in the refrigerator or several months in the freezer. See pages 54 and 88 for recipes that call for egg whites.

1 cup (8 oz/250 g) unsalted butter, at room temperature

1¼ cups (9 oz/280 g) firmly packed light brown sugar

2 tablespoons dark molasses

2 large egg yolks

½ teaspoon almond extract (essence)

3 cups (15 oz/470 g) all-purpose (plain) flour

2 teaspoons ground cinnamon

1 teaspoon ground cardamom

1 teaspoon baking soda (bicarbonate of soda)

¼ teaspoon salt

1 cup (4 oz/125 g) finely chopped unsalted pistachios

DOUBLE-GINGER SNAPS

2½ cups (12½ oz/390 g) all-purpose (plain) flour

1½ teaspoons ground ginger

1 teaspoon baking soda (bicarbonate of soda)

½ teaspoon ground cinnamon

¼ teaspoon ground cloves

¼ teaspoon salt

⅔ cup (5 fl oz/160 ml) canola oil

1 cup (7 oz/220 g) firmly packed light brown sugar

⅓ cup (3½ oz/105 g) dark molasses

1 large whole egg, lightly beaten, plus 1 large egg white

¾ cup (4½ oz/140 g) chopped crystallized ginger (far right)

½ cup (4 oz/125 g) coarse sugar crystals

Preheat the oven to 325°F (165°C). Lightly grease 2 baking sheets or line them with parchment (baking) paper.

Sift the flour, ground ginger, baking soda, cinnamon, cloves, and salt together onto a sheet of waxed paper.

In a large bowl, stir the oil, brown sugar, and molasses together with a wooden spoon until well blended. Add the whole egg and beat until blended. Stir in the flour mixture and crystallized ginger.

Lightly beat the egg white in a small bowl. Spread the sugar crystals in a shallow bowl.

With dampened hands, shape the dough into 1-inch (2.5-cm) balls. Brush each ball lightly with egg white and roll in the sugar to coat lightly. Place the cookies about 1 inch (2.5 cm) apart on the prepared pans.

Bake the cookies until the tops are set and crackled, 15–18 minutes. Let the cookies cool on the pans on wire racks for 5 minutes before transferring them to the racks to cool completely. The cookies will firm as they cool.

Make-Ahead Tip: These cookies keep well. Store between layers of waxed paper in an airtight container.

MAKES ABOUT 4 DOZEN COOKIES

CRYSTALLIZED GINGER

You can buy crystallized, or candied, ginger—or make it yourself at home. For homemade, bring 1½ cups (12 fl oz/375 ml) water to a boil. Stir in ½ cup (4 oz/125 g) sugar until dissolved. Cook over medium heat for 5 minutes, then add 1 cup (4 oz/125 g) thinly sliced (⅛ inch/3 mm), peeled fresh ginger. Reduce the heat to a simmer and cook until tender, about 10 minutes. Drain, then put the ginger in a bowl with ½ cup (4 oz/125 g) sugar and toss to coat. Spread out in a single layer on waxed paper and let cool. Store in a tightly covered jar for up to 3 weeks.

LIZZIES

Combine the raisins and brandy in a bowl and stir to blend. Cover and let plump for 1 hour. Toast the pecans, almonds, and Brazil nuts (page 22). When cool, chop coarsely and set aside.

Preheat the oven to 325°F (165°C). Lightly butter 2 baking sheets or line them with parchment (baking) paper.

In a large bowl, using an electric mixer on high speed, cream the butter until fluffy and pale yellow. Add the brown sugar and continue beating until the mixture is no longer gritty when rubbed between your finger and thumb. Add the eggs one at a time, beating well on low speed after each addition.

Sift the flour, baking soda, cinnamon, nutmeg, cloves, and salt together onto a sheet of waxed paper. Combine the nuts and all of the dried fruits, the cherries, and citron in a large bowl; add about ½ cup (2½ oz/75 g) of the flour mixture and toss to coat.

Add the remaining flour mixture to the butter mixture and mix on low speed or stir with a wooden spoon just until blended. Add the raisins and brandy and the fruit mixture and stir until blended.

Drop the batter by mounded teaspoons onto the prepared pans, spacing the cookies about 2 inches (5 cm) apart. Bake the cookies until set, about 15 minutes. Carefully transfer the cookies to wire racks to cool completely.

Using a fine-mesh sieve, dust the cookies with confectioners' sugar before serving.

Note: Lizzies are traditionally made only with candied fruit, but this version uses raisins and other dried fruits, such as apricots, prunes, pears, and figs, along with the typical candied citron or orange peel.

MAKES ABOUT 5 DOZEN COOKIES

PLUMPING DRIED FRUITS

Plumping raisins and other dried fruits softens them for eating and, if plumped in a spirit such as brandy or bourbon, adds flavor, too. Fruits are also sometimes plumped to make incorporating them into a batter easier, or, if they have become too hard, to regain their texture. The most common way to plump fruits is to immerse them in hot or warm water until they are rehydrated, typically about 20 minutes, and then drain them. When a spirit is used, its amount is usually specified, and then any remaining liquid is added to the batter as well.

2½ cups (15 oz/470 g) raisins

½ cup (4 fl oz/125 ml) brandy

2 cups (8 oz/250 g) pecan halves

1 cup (4 oz/125 g) *each* whole unblanched almonds and Brazil nuts

4 tablespoons (2 oz/60 g) unsalted butter, at room temperature

½ cup (3½ oz/105 g) firmly packed light brown sugar

2 large eggs

1½ cups (7½ oz/235 g) all-purpose (plain) flour

1½ teaspoons baking soda (bicarbonate of soda)

1½ teaspoons ground cinnamon

½ teaspoon *each* ground nutmeg and ground cloves

¼ teaspoon salt

3½ cups (1¼ lb/625 g) mixed dried fruits, snipped into ½-inch (12-mm) pieces

1 cup (6 oz/185 g) red candied cherries, halved

½ cup (3 oz/90 g) diced candied citron or orange peel

Confectioners' (icing) sugar for dusting

HAZELNUT AND DRIED CHERRY BISCOTTI

½ cup (4 oz/125 g)
unsalted butter, at room
temperature

¾ cup (6 oz/185 g) sugar

2 large eggs

2 teaspoons vanilla extract
(essence)

1¾ cups (9 oz/280 g)
all-purpose (plain) flour

½ teaspoon baking
powder

½ teaspoon ground
cinnamon

¼ teaspoon salt

1 cup (5 oz/155 g)
hazelnuts (filberts), toasted
and skinned (page 22),
then coarsely chopped

½ cup (3 oz/90 g) dried
tart cherries, coarsely
chopped

1 teaspoon grated
orange zest

Preheat the oven to 350°F (180°C). Lightly grease and flour 1 large baking sheet, or line it with parchment (baking) paper, and have another ungreased baking sheet on hand.

In a large bowl, using an electric mixer on high speed, cream the butter until fluffy and pale yellow. Add the sugar and continue beating until the mixture is no longer gritty when rubbed between your finger and thumb. Add the eggs one at a time, beating well on low speed after each addition. Beat in the vanilla on low speed until blended.

Sift the flour, baking powder, cinnamon, and salt together onto a sheet of waxed paper. Gradually add the flour mixture to the egg mixture and mix on low speed or stir with a wooden spoon just until incorporated. Mix or stir in the hazelnuts, cherries, and orange zest until evenly distributed. The batter should be very soft.

Turn the batter out onto a generously floured work surface and divide in half. With well-floured hands, transfer one-half onto the greased baking sheet and shape into a log about 12 inches (30 cm) long and 1½ inches (4 cm) in diameter. Place on one side of the sheet. Repeat with the remaining batter, leaving at least 4 inches (10 cm) between the logs. (They will spread as they bake.)

Bake the logs until the edges are golden, 25–30 minutes. Transfer the pan to a wire rack and let the logs cool for 10 minutes. Using a serrated knife, cut the logs, still on the pan, on the diagonal into slices ½ inch (12 mm) wide. Carefully turn the slices on their sides and return them to the oven. When you run out of room on one baking sheet, start transferring slices to the other sheet. Bake until the edges are golden, about 10 minutes longer. Let cool completely on the pans on wire racks. Store in an airtight container.

MAKES ABOUT 4 DOZEN BISCOTTI

ABOUT BISCOTTI

Biscotti means "twice baked" in Italian—and double baking is the secret to making these popular, crunchy cookies. To make biscotti, the dough is shaped into an oblong loaf and baked. The baked loaf is then cut into slices that are baked again until they become dry and hard. As durable as they are tasty, these cookies keep extremely well and are a good choice to give as a gift. They are delicious served with fresh fruit, and are perfect for dunking in coffee or a sweet dessert wine such as vin santo.

BUTTERSCOTCH COCONUT COOKIES

SHREDDED COCONUT

Growing on palm trees in tropical climates, the coconut is the world's largest nut. Its nutmeat is firm, creamy, and snowy white and is a favorite ingredient for sweet baked goods. Bags of shredded dried coconut are available in the baking supply aisles of most supermarkets. Shredded dried coconut is almost always sweetened, but it is possible to buy it unsweetened. Check the bag and your recipe to make sure you have the correct type.

Preheat the oven to 325°F (165°C). Have ready 2 baking sheets lined with parchment (baking) paper

Sift the flour, baking powder, baking   together onto a sheet of waxed paper; set aside.

In a large bowl, using an electric mixer on high speed, cream the butter until fluffy and pale yellow. Add the granulated and brown sugars and continue beating until the mixture is no longer gritty when rubbed between your finger and thumb. Add the egg and vanilla and beat on low speed until blended, occasionally stopping the mixer and scraping down the sides of the bowl with a rubber spatula as needed.

Add the flour mixture to the butter mixture and mix on low speed or stir with a wooden spoon just until blended. Add the coconut and butterscotch chips, mixing or stirring just until blended.

With dampened hands, shape the dough into 1-inch (2.5-cm) balls or drop by rounded tablespoons onto the prepared baking sheets, spacing the cookies about 2 inches (5 cm) apart.

Bake the cookies until golden brown around the edges, about 15 minutes. Let the cookies cool briefly on the pans on wire racks before transferring them to the racks to cool completely.

MAKES ABOUT 4 DOZEN COOKIES

1⅓ cups (7 oz/220 g) all-purpose (plain) flour

½ teaspoon baking powder

½ teaspoon baking soda (bicarbonate of soda)

½ teaspoon salt

½ cup (4 oz/125 g) unsalted butter, at room temperature

½ cup (4 oz/125 g) granulated sugar

½ cup (3½ oz/105 g) firmly packed light brown sugar

1 large egg

½ teaspoon vanilla extract (essence)

1¾ cups (7 oz/220 g) sweetened shredded dried coconut

1½ cups (9 oz/280 g) butterscotch chips

OATMEAL, DATE, AND WALNUT SPICE COOKIES

2 cups (10 oz/315 g)
all-purpose (plain) flour

1 teaspoon baking powder

½ teaspoon baking soda
(bicarbonate of soda)

½ teaspoon salt

1 teaspoon ground
cinnamon

½ teaspoon freshly grated
nutmeg

¼ teaspoon ground allspice

1 cup (8 oz/250 g)
unsalted butter, at
room temperature

½ cup (3½ oz/105 g) firmly
packed light brown sugar

½ cup (4 oz/125 g)
granulated sugar

2 large eggs

3 tablespoons dark
molasses

1½ teaspoons vanilla
extract (essence)

2½ cups (7½ oz/235 g)
old-fashioned rolled oats

1 cup (6 oz/185 g)
chopped pitted dates

½ cup (2 oz/60 g) coarsely
chopped walnuts

Coarse sugar crystals for
sprinkling (optional)

Preheat the oven to 375°F (190°C). Lightly grease 2 baking sheets or line them with parchment (baking) paper.

Sift the flour, baking powder, baking soda, salt, and spices together onto a sheet of waxed paper; set aside.

In a large bowl, using an electric mixer on high speed, cream the butter until fluffy and pale yellow. Add the brown and granulated sugars and continue beating until the mixture is no longer gritty when rubbed between your finger and thumb. Add the eggs one at a time, beating well on low speed after each addition. Beat in the molasses and vanilla.

Add the flour mixture and mix on low speed or stir with a wooden spoon just until blended. Mix or stir in the rolled oats, dates, and walnuts just until evenly distributed.

Drop the batter by rounded tablespoons onto the prepared pans, spacing the cookies about 2 inches (5 cm) apart. Bake the cookies until the edges are golden, 10–12 minutes. If desired, sprinkle the cookies with coarse sugar while they are still warm. Let the cookies cool on the pans on wire racks for 10 minutes before transferring them to wire racks to cool completely.

MAKES ABOUT 4 DOZEN COOKIES

ALLSPICE

The berry of an evergreen tree, allspice tastes like a combination of cinnamon, nutmeg, and cloves. It is a particular favorite with holiday bakers, who like to add its bold flavor to cookies, cakes, and pies. Allspice can be used ground or whole. Buy allspice, especially ground allspice, in the smallest amount you can from a store with high turnover, as it will begin to lose its flavor after 6 months. If possible, purchase allspice in bulk, buying only a little at a time. If you buy a can or jar, be sure to check it for a date to ensure freshness.

COCONUT-MACADAMIA TRIANGLES

Preheat the oven to 375°F (190°C). Line the bottom and sides of a 9-inch (23-cm) square pan with aluminum foil and lightly grease the foil.

Combine the 1 cup flour, the 1 tablespoon brown sugar, and ½ teaspoon of the salt in a food processor. Process briefly to blend. With the motor running, add the butter a few pieces at a time until small crumbs form. Turn out into the prepared pan. Press the mixture into the pan in an even, solid layer.

Bake until the edges are golden, about 10 minutes.

Meanwhile, combine the 2 tablespoons flour, the ¾ cup brown sugar, the corn syrup, vanilla, egg, and the remaining ¼ teaspoon salt. Beat with a wooden spoon until thoroughly blended. Stir in the nuts and coconut until blended.

Spread the coconut topping over the warm baked bottom crust. Return to the oven and bake until the topping is lightly browned and the edges pull away from the sides of the pan, 15–20 minutes. Let cool completely in the pan on a wire rack. Lift out the foil to remove the cookie from the pan.

Cut the cookie into twelve 3-by-2¼-inch (7.5-by-5.5-cm) rectangles. Cut each rectangle in half on the diagonal to make triangles. Dip 1 corner of each triangle in the melted chocolate and let cool on a sheet of waxed paper.

MAKES 2 DOZEN COOKIES

MACADAMIA NUTS

Macadamia nuts add natural sweetness and a buttery flavor to baked goods. Usually sold shelled, they taste slightly sweet, and have a smooth, creamy texture. Like many nuts, their high fat content makes them prone to rancidity, so purchase them in a store that has good turnover to ensure that they are as fresh as possible. Store shelled nuts in an airtight container for 1 to 2 months at room temperature, 3 to 6 months in the refrigerator, or 9 months to 1 year in the freezer in a heavy-duty zippered plastic bag.

1 cup (5 oz/155 g) plus 2 tablespoons all-purpose (plain) flour

¾ cup (6 oz/185 g) firmly packed light brown sugar, plus 1 tablespoon

¾ teaspoon salt

5 tablespoons (2½ oz/ 75 g) cold unsalted butter, cut into small pieces

2 tablespoons light corn syrup

1 teaspoon vanilla extract (essence)

1 large egg

1 cup (5 oz/155 g) unsalted macadamia nuts, lightly toasted (page 22) and coarsely chopped

½ cup (2 oz/60 g) shredded sweetened dried coconut

3 oz (90 g) semisweet (plain) chocolate, melted (page 50)

HOLIDAY COOKIES

The aroma of freshly baked cookies is especially enticing during the holidays. Treat yourself to traditional cinnamon rugelach or indulgent bourbon balls, or expand your holiday repertoire with Moravian molasses cookies spiced with ginger and allspice. Whether you stick with the classics or try something new, a platter of sweet treats will add to the pleasure of the season.

SPRITZ COOKIES

Preheat the oven to 375°F (190°C). Then set out 2 ungreased baking sheets.

In a large bowl, using an electric mixer on high speed, cream the butter until fluffy and pale yellow. Add the granulated sugar and continue beating until the mixture is no longer gritty when rubbed between your finger and thumb. Beat in the egg yolks and vanilla and almond extracts on low speed just until blended.

Sift the flour and salt together onto a sheet of waxed paper. Add the flour mixture to the butter mixture and mix on low speed or stir with a wooden spoon just until blended.

Fill a cookie press with dough following the manufacturer's instructions. Press the cookies out directly onto the pans. (Any piped dough that doesn't come out neatly may be scraped off the baking sheet and put through the press again.) If the dough becomes too warm and sticky, refrigerate it for a few minutes to firm it up.

Lightly brush each cookie with egg white, and sprinkle with sugar or sprinkles or press a candied cherry in the center of each. Bake just until the edges are golden, 8–10 minutes. (If the shapes don't hold their definition after baking, refrigerate the dough for the next batch for 20 minutes to firm it up before pressing.) Let the cookies cool on the pan on wire racks for 1–2 minutes to set before transferring them to wire racks to cool completely.

Preparation Tip: Make sure to press cookies onto cool (never warm) baking sheets. The dough won't adhere properly to warm sheets, and the cookies will slip when you pull the press away.

MAKES ABOUT 5 DOZEN COOKIES

1 cup (8 oz/250 g) unsalted butter, at room temperature

¾ cup (6 oz/185 g) granulated sugar

2 large egg yolks

1 teaspoon vanilla extract (essence)

½ teaspoon almond extract (essence)

2¼ cups (11 oz/345 g) all-purpose (plain) flour

¼ teaspoon salt

1 egg white, lightly beaten

Granulated or colored sugar, sprinkles, or red or green glacéed cherries (optional)

USING A COOKIE PRESS

Equipped with a selection of plates to create different shapes, a cookie press makes it easy to turn out batch after batch of beautiful cookies. Before using the press, roll the cookie dough inside a sheet of waxed paper into a log slightly smaller in size than the cylinder on the cookie press. Remove the paper, slip the dough into the cylinder, select the design plate you desire, and screw it securely into place. Hold the press upright, tightly grasp the handle, and, applying even pressure, press out the dough to form cookies. Cookie presses work best with a fairly soft, pliable dough.

MEXICAN WEDDING COOKIES

1 cup (8 oz/250 g) unsalted butter, at room temperature

1¼ cups (5 oz/150 g) confectioners' (icing) sugar

1 teaspoon vanilla extract (essence)

¼ teaspoon salt

1¾ cups (9 oz/280 g) all-purpose (plain) flour

1 teaspoon ground cinnamon

1 cup (5 oz/155 g) ground blanched almonds

In a large bowl, using an electric mixer on high speed, cream the butter until fluffy and pale yellow. Add ½ cup (2 oz/60 g) of the confectioners' sugar and continue beating until light and fluffy. Add the vanilla and salt and beat on low speed until blended.

Sift the flour and cinnamon together onto a sheet of waxed paper. Add the flour mixture to the butter mixture and mix on low speed or stir with a wooden spoon just until blended. Stir in the almonds. Cover and refrigerate until the dough is chilled, but not hard, and is no longer sticky to the touch, about 15 minutes.

Preheat the oven to 350°F (180°C). Have ready 2 ungreased baking sheets. Sift the remaining ¾ cup (3 oz/90 g) confectioners' sugar into a shallow bowl.

Shape the dough into 1-inch (2.5-cm) balls. Place about 1 inch (2.5 cm) apart on the baking sheets.

Bake the cookies until just golden on the bottom, 10–12 minutes. Let the cookies cool on the pans on wire racks for 5 minutes before removing them one at a time and rolling them in the sugar. Let cool completely on wire racks.

MAKES ABOUT 4 DOZEN COOKIES

USING SPICES

Spices get their flavors from essential oils that evaporate over time, so they need to be replaced periodically. If stored in tightly closed containers in a cool, dark place, ground spices will last for about 6 months and whole spices will last for about 1 year. Purchase spices in small amounts from stores with high turnover. For the most pronounced flavor, use whole spices and grind them fresh. To grind the cinnamon for this recipe, toast part of a cinnamon stick in a small frying pan over medium heat until fragrant, then break up and grind in a mortar with a pestle or in a spice grinder.

MORAVIAN MOLASSES COOKIES

In a large bowl, using an electric mixer on high speed, cream the butter until fluffy and pale yellow. Beat in the brown sugar until no longer gritty when rubbed between your finger and thumb. Gradually beat in the molasses on low speed.

Sift the flour, baking soda, baking powder, cinnamon, ginger, and allspice together onto a sheet of waxed paper. Add the flour mixture to the butter mixture in 3 additions, mixing on low speed or stirring with a wooden spoon after each addition until well blended.

Turn the dough out onto a lightly floured surface and divide into 6 equal portions. Form each into a flattened disk, wrap in plastic wrap, and refrigerate for at least 2 hours or for up to overnight.

When ready to bake, preheat the oven to 350°F (180°C). Lightly grease 2 baking sheets or line them with parchment (baking) paper.

Working with 1 portion at a time, roll out the dough on a floured surface to a thickness of about ⅛ inch (3 mm). Using a 2-inch (5-cm) fluted or plain cookie cutter, cut out shapes or rounds. Using a thin offset spatula, carefully transfer to the prepared pans, brushing off excess flour and placing the cookies about 1 inch (2.5 cm) apart. Repeat with the remaining dough, then gather up the scraps, reroll them, and cut out additional cookies. If desired, sprinkle each cookie with some of the cinnamon-sugar mixture.

Bake the cookies until set, 6–8 minutes. Let the cookies cool on the pans on wire racks for about 2 minutes. Using a thin, flexible metal spatula, transfer them to the racks to cool completely.

Notes: The dough for these delicate, full-flavored cookies is easy to handle, so don't be afraid to roll it out thinly. These delicious spice cookies are a traditional treat at Christmastime in Moravia, a region that is today part of the Czech Republic.

MAKES ABOUT 6 DOZEN COOKIES

MOLASSES

A thick, robust-tasting syrup, molasses is a by-product of cane-sugar refining. Each step in the molasses-making process produces a different type of molasses. Mixed with pure cane syrup, light molasses has the lightest flavor and color. Dark molasses is thicker, darker, stronger in flavor, and less sweet than light molasses. Almost all molasses sold today is unsulfured. Sulfur was once regularly added to help clarify the cane liquids during sugar processing, but its use has largely ended because of a high incidence of allergic reaction.

½ cup (4 oz/125 g) unsalted butter, at room temperature

½ cup (3½ oz/105 g) firmly packed dark brown sugar

⅔ cup (7½ oz/230 g) dark molasses

2½ cups (12½ oz/390 g) all-purpose (plain) flour

1 teaspoon baking soda (bicarbonate of soda)

½ teaspoon baking powder

1 teaspoon ground cinnamon

1 teaspoon ground ginger

¼ teaspoon ground allspice

2 teaspoons granulated sugar mixed with ¼ teaspoon ground cinnamon for sprinkling (optional)

BRANDY SNAPS

½ cup (5½ oz/170 g) light molasses

½ cup (4 oz/125 g) unsalted butter

1¼ cups (4 oz/125 g) sifted cake (soft-wheat) flour

⅔ cup (5 oz/155 g) sugar

1 teaspoon ground cinnamon

¼ teaspoon salt

2 tablespoons brandy

Preheat the oven to 350°F (180°C). Generously grease 2 baking sheets or line them with parchment (baking) paper. Have ready a slender rolling pin or wooden dowel ¾ inch (2 cm) in diameter.

In a small saucepan, bring the molasses to a boil over low heat. Add the butter and stir to melt. Remove from the heat.

Sift the sifted flour, sugar, cinnamon, and salt together onto a sheet of waxed paper. Stir the flour mixture into the butter mixture with a wooden spoon until blended. Stir in the brandy. The batter should be thick and syrupy.

Drop the batter by heaping teaspoons onto the prepared pans, spacing the cookies about 3 inches (7.5 cm) apart and forming only 6 cookies. (The cookies must be baked in small batches, because, once baked, they must be shaped quickly before they cool and become brittle.)

Bake the cookies until they spread out and the surface is bubbly, 5–7 minutes. Let cool on the pan on a wire rack for just 1 minute, then, working quickly, use a thin, flexible metal spatula to remove 1 cookie at a time and wrap it around the rolling pin or dowel, placing the flat side of the cookie against the dowel, to make a hollow tube. Let the cookie set until it holds this shape. Use several dowels to shape as many cookies at one time as possible. If the cookies become too cool to shape easily, return them to the oven for a few moments; they will soften from the heat.

While the next batch bakes, slip the set cookies from the dowels to a wire rack. Let all the cookies cool to room temperature, then fill if desired *(right)* and serve.

Make-Ahead Tip: These cookies may be stored for several days in an airtight container, then filled just before serving.

MAKES ABOUT 4 DOZEN COOKIES

CREAM FILLING

If you are feeling indulgent, fill these cylindrical cookies with freshly whipped cream. Chill heavy (double) cream well, then stir in 2 tablespoons confectioners' (icing) sugar and 1 tablespoon brandy. Beat in a chilled, deep bowl with a whisk or an electric mixer just until soft peaks form. Do not overbeat, or the cream will turn into butter. Once whipped, the cream will hold for 30 minutes or so, covered, in the refrigerator. Use a pastry bag fitted with a large, plain tip (page 53) to fill the cookies. Arrange on a platter and serve at once.

BOURBON BALLS

Finely crush the vanilla wafers in batches in a food processor, or place them in a heavy-duty plastic bag and crush them with a rolling pin.

Melt the chocolate in the top of a double boiler (page 50) over barely simmering water. Remove from the heat and add the brown sugar, corn syrup, bourbon, and salt; stir to blend. Stir in the crushed vanilla wafers and half of the pecans.

Spread the remaining pecans on a plate. Using your hands, shape the dough into 1-inch (2.5-cm) balls. Roll the balls in the nuts to coat evenly. Arrange the balls in layers, separated by waxed paper, in a tightly covered container. Refrigerate for 24 hours before serving, to blend the flavors.

Make-Ahead Tip: These cookies will keep, refrigerated, for up to 2 weeks.

MAKES ABOUT 4½ DOZEN COOKIES

1 box (12 oz/375 g) vanilla wafers, broken into pieces

6 oz (185 g) semisweet (plain) chocolate, finely chopped

½ cup (3½ oz/105 g) firmly packed light brown sugar

¼ cup (2½ fl oz/75 ml) light corn syrup

⅓ cup (3 fl oz/80 ml) bourbon

Pinch of salt

2 cups (8 oz/250 g) pecans, lightly toasted (page 22), then finely chopped

PECANS

Native to North America, the pecan has two deeply crinkled lobes of nutmeat, much like its relative the walnut. The nuts have smooth, brown, oval shells that break easily, making them good candidates for buying whole and shelling yourself. Raw, unshelled nuts have a longer shelf life than shelled nuts, and keep well for 6 months to 1 year if stored away from light, heat, and moisture. Since nuts contain high amounts of oil, they will eventually turn rancid, so check them for freshness before adding to recipes.

RUGELACH WITH APRICOT AND PISTACHIO FILLING

¼ lb (125 g) cream cheese, cut into small pieces, at room temperature

½ cup (4 oz/125 g) unsalted butter, cut into small pieces, at room temperature

1 cup (5 oz/155 g) plus 2 tablespoons unbleached all-purpose (plain) flour

2 tablespoons granulated sugar

¼ teaspoon salt

FOR THE FILLING:

¾ cup (4 oz/125 g) dried apricots, halved

1 tablespoon granulated sugar

¼ teaspoon ground cinnamon

2 tablespoons finely chopped unsalted pistachios

Confectioners' (icing) sugar for dusting

Combine the cream cheese, butter, flour, granulated sugar, and salt in a food processor. Pulse just until the dough begins to clump together. Turn the dough out onto a floured work surface and gather into a ball. Divide into 4 equal portions. Place each portion on a piece of plastic wrap, flatten slightly into a disk, wrap, and refrigerate for at least 2 hours or for up to 6 hours.

Meanwhile, make the filling. In a small saucepan, combine the apricots and ½ cup (4 fl oz/125 ml) water. Cover and cook over low heat, stirring occasionally, until the fruit absorbs the water, 10–15 minutes. Let cool slightly, then transfer to the food processor and process to a fairly smooth purée. Pour into a bowl and stir in the granulated sugar, cinnamon, and pistachios. Set aside.

Preheat the oven to 350°F (180°C). Line 2 baking sheets with parchment (baking) paper.

Lightly flour a work surface. Remove 1 disk of dough from the refrigerator and roll into a 7-inch (18-cm) circle *(right)*. Spread one-fourth of the filling evenly over the top. With a large knife, cut the dough into 6 wedges. Starting at the outside edge, gently roll up each wedge toward the point. (If needed, use a thin metal spatula to loosen the wedges from the work surface.) If the dough becomes too soft to roll, refrigerate for about 5 minutes to firm up. As each piece is formed, place it at least 1 inch (2.5 cm) apart on the prepared baking sheets; bend the ends of the dough toward the center to form a crescent shape. Repeat with remaining dough and filling, flouring the work surface as needed.

Bake the rugelach until golden brown, about 20 minutes. Let cool on the pans on wire racks for 5 minutes before transferring to the racks to cool completely. While still warm, use a fine-mesh sieve to dust the rugelach with confectioners' sugar.

MAKES ABOUT 2½ DOZEN COOKIES

ROLLING OUT DOUGH
To roll out dough, use a marble or wooden pin. Roll from the center toward the outside edge, using short, firm strokes and stopping just shy of the edge to keep it from becoming too thin. After each roll, rotate the dough a quarter turn to prevent it from sticking to the work surface. Lightly dust the surface and rolling pin with more flour as needed. Beginners may find it easier to roll dough out between 2 sheets of waxed paper, which prevents sticking and tearing.

HAZELNUT MERINGUES

Preheat the oven to 275°F (135°C). Line 2 baking sheets with aluminum foil or parchment (baking) paper.

Sift the superfine sugar, cream of tartar, cinnamon, ginger, and salt together on a sheet of waxed paper; set aside.

In a large bowl, combine the egg whites and vanilla. Using an electric mixer on medium speed (or a whisk), beat until soft and foamy. Increase the speed and, while continuing to beat, add the sugar mixture a little at a time, beating until stiff, glossy peaks form *(left)*, 3–4 minutes. Using a rubber spatula, fold in ¾ cup (3 oz/90 g) of the chopped hazelnuts.

Using a pastry bag with a large, plain tip, pipe the meringue onto the prepared pans, forming drops ¾–1 inch (2–2.5 cm) in diameter and spacing them about ½ inch (12 mm) apart. Alternatively, drop the meringue from the tip of a teaspoon to make bite-sized shapes. Sprinkle a few of the remaining nuts on top of each meringue.

Bake the meringues until lightly colored, 25–30 minutes. Turn off the oven and prop open the oven door about 1 inch (2.5 cm). Let cool completely, about 2 hours.

Note: This is a good recipe for using up leftover egg whites. Whites can be stored, tightly covered, in the refrigerator for up to 5 days or frozen for several months.

MAKES 60-70 MERINGUES

¾ cup (6 oz/185 g) superfine (caster) sugar

½ teaspoon cream of tartar

¼ teaspoon ground cinnamon

⅛ teaspoon ground ginger

Pinch of salt

4 large egg whites, at room temperature

1 teaspoon vanilla extract (essence)

1¼ cups (6½ oz/200 g) hazelnuts (filberts), toasted and skinned (page 22), then finely chopped

BEATING EGG WHITES

Recipes that call for beating egg whites usually include cream of tartar, a powdery white by-product of wine making that helps keep the whites foamy. (A copper bowl, which also stabilizes the foam, may be used instead.) Begin beating with an electric mixer on medium-low speed. When soft and foamy but still loose, increase the speed. The whites will grow thick and shiny as you beat. To test for stiffness, lift the beaters. If peaks on the beaters' tips fall gently to one side, they are soft; if they hold their shape, they are stiff. You can also use a whisk to beat egg whites by hand.

DECORATED COOKIES

From crisp sugar cookies sprinkled with colorful sugars to gingerbread men dressed up in bright icing, decorating turns cookie making into an art. As delicious to eat as they are fun to create, these fanciful, eye catching treats bring cheer to occasions throughout the year.

DECORATING WITH ICING

Using a decorative cookie cutter, cut out and bake the cookies as directed, omitting the sugar topping. Let cool completely.

To color the icing, divide it among separate small bowls, one for each color desired. Add only a drop or so of a different food coloring to each bowl *(left)*. Stir until completely blended. Repeat as needed to create the desired color. To decorate:

Flowing Icing: Using a pastry bag fitted with a narrow tip (page 53), outline the edges of a cookie with the icing, then use a small, damp pastry brush to flow (spread) an even, solid layer of icing within the outline. You may need to thin the icing with a few drops of water to help it flow. For a perfectly smooth finish, use the tip of a wooden skewer to pop any bubbles that develop on the icing's surface. Let set completely; this will take 1–3 hours, depending on the humidity.

Layering Icing: After flowing an initial layer of icing *(above)* and allowing it to set completely, use the pastry bag or a brush to apply an additional decorative layer of icing, in the same color or a different one as desired *(see spider and ghosts, right)*. Let set completely.

Star Burst: Flow a layer of icing over a cookie *(above)*. While the icing layer is still wet, use a different color of icing in another pastry bag fitted with a narrow tip to pipe a dot in the center of the cookie and then surround it with a series of concentric circles. Starting in the center, use a toothpick or wooden skewer to draw a straight line to the edge of the cookie. Repeat to create a star burst pattern *(see spiderweb, right)*. Let set completely.

MAKES 2–3 DOZEN COOKIES, DEPENDING ON SIZE

1 recipe Sugar Cookies
(page 14)

FOR THE DECORATIONS:
1 recipe Royal Icing
(page 99)

Food coloring liquid, gel, or paste, as needed *(far left)*

COLORING THE ICING

To add color to Royal Icing, stir food coloring into a small dish of icing. Start with a drop or two of coloring and add more as needed to deepen the color. Bottles of liquid food coloring are available in the baking aisle of every supermarket, but other types of food coloring may be found in specialty-food shops. Food color gels and pastes create more intense and unusual colors and won't water down the icing as much. Also, natural food dyes are becoming available in a pretty palette of muted colors, such as sage green and pumpkin-pie orange.

DECORATING WITH SUGAR

1 recipe Sugar Cookies
(page 14)

FOR THE DECORATIONS:

1 recipe Royal Icing
(page 99) (optional)

1 large egg white, lightly
beaten (see Note), or
2 teaspoons meringue
powder mixed with
2 tablespoons water

Assorted colored
decorating sugars
(far right)

Using a decorative cookie cutter, cut out and bake the cookies as directed, omitting the sugar topping. Let cool completely.

To color the icing, divide it among separate small bowls, one for each color desired. Add only a drop or so of a different food coloring to each bowl (page 92). Stir until completely blended. Repeat as needed to create the desired color. To decorate:

Sugar: Brush a cookie with egg white and dip into a dish of colored sugar. Once the sugar is dry, use a pastry bag to pipe decorations with Royal Icing, if desired (page 53) *(see purple flower, left)*. Let set completely.

Icing and Sugar: Using a pastry bag fitted with a narrow tip, outline the edges of a cookie with icing, then use a small, damp pastry brush to flow (spread) an even, solid layer of icing within the cookie outline. You may need to thin the icing with a few drops of water to help it flow. Alternatively, use a pastry bag to pipe patterns of icing. While the icing is still wet, use a small spoon to sprinkle the icing with sugar, then invert the cookie briefly to let the excess sugar fall off *(see blue butterfly, left)*. Let set completely.

Layered Icing and Sugar: Use a pastry bag and brush to flow a thin layer of icing onto a cookie *(as above)*. Let the layer set completely, 1–3 hours. After the icing has set, use the pastry bag or a brush to add an additional decorative layer of icing in the same or another color. While this second layer of icing is still wet, use a small spoon to sprinkle the icing with sugar, then invert the cookie briefly to let the excess fall off *(see flowerpot and yellow butterfly, left)*. Let set completely.

Note: This recipe uses uncooked egg whites. For more information, see pages 113–14.

MAKES 2–3 DOZEN COOKIES, DEPENDING ON SIZE

DECORATING SUGARS

Colored sugars give these cookies a beautiful sparkle. An assortment of different colors are available, from delicate pastels to more assertive hues. Colored sugars are also sold in different-sized grains, from fine to coarse. The coarser the sugar, the more the final cookie will sparkle. Most well-stocked supermarkets carry colored sugars, but for a wider selection, look in cake-decorating and pastry-supply stores. Using a solid layer of Royal Icing in the same color as a decorating sugar creates a pretty effect, boosting the color of the sugar.

DECORATING WITH PIPED ICING

Using a decorative cookie cutter, cut out and bake the cookies as directed, omitting the sugar topping. Let cool completely.

To color the icing, divide it among separate small bowls, one for each color desired. Add only a drop or so of a different food coloring to each bowl (page 92). Stir until completely blended. Repeat as needed to create the desired color.

For a solid layer of icing on a cookie, using a pastry bag fitted with a narrow tip (page 53), outline the edges of a cookie with icing, then use a small, damp pastry brush to flow (spread) icing within the outline. You may need to thin the icing with a few drops of water to help it flow. If using decorating sugar, while the icing is still wet, use a small spoon to sprinkle the icing with sugar, then invert the cookie briefly to let the excess sugar fall off. Let the icing set completely, 1–3 hours depending on the humidity, before piping on decorative patterns. Keep the remaining icing in an airtight container while waiting for the first layer to set. To decorate:

Beading: Hold a pastry bag fitted with a narrow tip perpendicular to the cookie and squeeze the bag gently to create a small drop of icing. Repeat to make a beaded pattern *(see dark blue star, right).* Let set completely.

Lines: Hold the pastry bag at a 45-degree angle to the cookie and squeeze the bag gently and evenly to pipe icing lines onto the cookie *(see light blue star and snowflakes, right).*

While the piped icing is still wet, use clean tweezers to apply sprinkles, beads, dragées, or other decorations as desired. Let set completely.

Decorating Tip: Inserting a toothpick or wooden skewer will help clear a clogged pastry bag tip.

MAKES 2–3 DOZEN COOKIES, DEPENDING ON SIZE

PIPING SHORTCUT

With a little practice, piping with a pastry bag is quite simple—but there is an easier way. Look for decorating pens in specialty-food and baking-supply shops. Pens offer less control than regular piping because the pens are heated in warm water before use and the line of icing thickens as it cools, but they are a good choice for decorating with children. If you are caught with neither a pastry bag nor a decorating pen, use a heavy-gauge plastic bag with one corner snipped off as a makeshift pastry bag.

1 recipe Sugar Cookies (page 14)

FOR THE DECORATIONS:
1 recipe Royal Icing (page 99)

Assorted colored decorating sugars (optional)

Sprinkles, beads, dragées, or other decorations (optional)

GINGERBREAD MEN

GINGERBREAD
DECORATIONS

Silvery or pearlescent
dragées in a variety of sizes,
small red or white candies,
and colored sprinkles can
dress up any gingerbread
man (or woman). After the
baked cookies have cooled,
decorate with icing and use
clean tweezers to place the
desired decorations on the
still-wet icing. For a more
homey look, while the cookies
are still warm, press dried
currants, dried cranberries, or
raisins down the center of
each torso to make buttons.
Or, before baking, use a clean
garlic press to make
gingerbread hair.

In a large bowl, using an electric mixer on high speed, cream the butter until fluffy and pale yellow. Add the brown and granulated sugars and beat until the mixture no longer feels gritty when rubbed between your thumb and forefinger. Gradually beat in the molasses on low speed. Add the egg and beat on low speed until the mixture is blended.

Sift the flour, baking soda, ginger, cinnamon, cloves, and salt together onto a sheet of waxed paper. Gradually add the flour mixture to the butter mixture, mixing on low speed or stirring with a wooden spoon until well blended. Turn out onto a floured work surface and, with floured hands, form into a large, smooth mound. Divide the dough into 4 equal portions, shape into disks, and wrap each disk in plastic wrap. Refrigerate for at least 2 hours or for up to 2 days.

Preheat the oven to 400°F (200°C). Lightly grease 2 baking sheets or line with parchment (baking) paper. Working with 1 disk at a time, roll out the dough between 2 sheets of waxed paper to a thickness of about ¼ inch (6 mm). Using gingerbread cookie cutters 3–5 inches (7.5–13 cm) tall, cut out figures. Use an offset spatula to transfer to a prepared pan. Repeat with the remaining dough portions, then gather up the scraps, reroll them, and cut out additional cookies. If the scraps of dough have become sticky, refrigerate them for 10 minutes before rerolling. For best results, do not roll the same dough more than twice.

Bake the gingerbread figures until lightly browned on the bottom, about 6 minutes. Let sit on the sheets for 5 minutes before transferring to wire racks to cool completely. Dress up the cooled gingerbread figures with icing (pages 92 and 96), sugars (page 95), and other decorations *(left)*.

MAKES 2–5 DOZEN COOKIES, DEPENDING ON SIZE

1 cup (8 oz/250 g)
unsalted butter, at
room temperature

½ cup (3½ oz/105 g)
firmly packed light brown
sugar

½ cup (4 oz/125 g)
granulated sugar

1 cup (11 oz/345 g) light
molasses

1 large egg

5 cups (25 oz/780 g)
all-purpose (plain) flour

1 teaspoon baking soda
(bicarbonate of soda)

1 tablespoon ground
ginger

1 teaspoon ground
cinnamon

½ teaspoon ground cloves

½ teaspoon salt

ROYAL ICING

FOR THE ROYAL ICING WITH EGG:

3 large egg whites, at room temperature

¼ teaspoon cream of tartar

4 cups (1 lb/500 g) confectioners' (icing) sugar, sifted

FOR THE ROYAL ICING WITHOUT EGG:

3 tablespoons meringue powder

6 tablespoons (3 fl oz/ 90 ml) warm water, plus more as needed

4 cups (1 lb/500 g) confectioners' (icing) sugar, sifted

To make Royal Icing with egg *(right),* in a large bowl and using a mixer on medium speed, beat the egg whites with the cream of tartar until foamy. Reduce the mixer speed to low and gradually beat in the confectioners' sugar until blended, then beat on high speed until thick and glossy, about 2 minutes.

To make Royal Icing without egg, in a large bowl and using a mixer on medium speed, combine the meringue powder and 6 tablespoons warm water. Reduce the mixer speed to low and gradually beat in the confectioners' sugar until blended, then beat on high speed until very thick and smooth, about 5 minutes. Beat in more warm water, 1 tablespoon at a time, if the icing is too thick to spread or pipe.

To use the icing for decorating the gingerbread figures or other cookies, see the techniques on pages 92–96.

MAKES ABOUT 2 CUPS (16 FL OZ/500 ML)

ABOUT ROYAL ICING

Royal Icing is the classic icing used to decorate cookies for any occasion. Its consistency can easily be altered with warm water if it is too thick to spread or with additional confectioners' sugar if it is too thin to pipe. Keep icing tightly covered while you work, as it dries out quickly. Classic Royal Icing contains raw egg, which can be a health risk. For more information, see pages 113–14. If you have health and safety concerns, use the egg-free variation.

DECORATING WITH APPLIQUÉS

Sugar Cookie dough
(page 14), chilled

FOR THE FILLING:

3–4 tablespoons seedless
jelly or jam such as
apricot, red currant, or
raspberry, or a
combination

3–4 tablespoons purchased
lemon curd

Line 2 baking sheets with parchment (baking) paper. Divide the dough into 4 equal portions and let stand at room temperature for about 15 minutes. To make the cookie bottoms, roll out 1 portion on a lightly floured work surface to a thickness of ⅛ inch (3 mm). Using a floured 2¼-inch (5.5-cm) square cookie cutter, cut into squares. Using an offset spatula, transfer them to the prepared pans. Repeat with another dough portion, then reroll the scraps and cut out additional squares. If the scraps of dough have become sticky, refrigerate them for 10 minutes before rerolling.

To make the appliqué tops, roll out another dough portion. Use the same square cutter to cut into squares. Repeat with the remaining dough portion, then reroll the scraps and cut out additional squares. Dip miniature cookie cutters in flour and cut out patterns in half of the tops, flouring with each cut and using the blunt end of a small skewer to push out the tiny shapes, if necessary. Use a smaller 1½-inch (4-cm) square cutter to make windows in the remaining tops. Transfer all the cutout tops, windowed tops, and cutout shapes to the prepared pans.

Cover the pans and place in the freezer for 30 minutes. Preheat the oven to 350°F (180°C).

Bake the cookies until lightly golden, about 10 minutes for the bottom cookies, 5–7 minutes for the cutout tops. Let cool briefly on the pans before transferring to wire racks to cool completely. Meanwhile, in 1 or more small saucepans (if using more than one jelly or jam), over low heat, warm the jelly or jam, stirring until slightly thinned. Lemon curd need not be warmed.

Spread the cookie bottoms with a thin layer (about 1 teaspoon) of jelly or lemon curd to within about ¼ inch (6 mm) of the edges. Top with the appliqué tops and shapes.

MAKES 1½–2 DOZEN COOKIES

MINIATURE COOKIE
CUTTERS

At one time, miniature cutters such as those pictured above were most often used for cutting aspic. But today, a whole assortment of such cutters is available for making decorative cookies, as this recipe demonstrates. A variety of shapes can be found, such as diamonds, hearts, clovers, and even tiny letters. Look for assorted cutters sold in tins in cookware stores. If you don't have miniature cookie cutters, use a floured small, sharp knife to cut out free-form shapes or initials.

COOKIE BASICS

Cookies come in just about every shape and flavor you can imagine: rich chocolate brownies, thin nut slices, jam-filled sandwiches, crisp tuiles, delicate sugar-dusted rounds, bourbon-laced balls. Generally easy to make and always guaranteed to please, cookies can be enjoyed anytime. Whether served with a cup of tea after dinner, tucked away in a lunchbox, or sent in a gift package to a friend far away, cookies are just what we need to satisfy our craving for a little something sweet.

GETTING STARTED

Before you start making any cookie recipe, read the ingredients list and the directions carefully. Make sure you understand every step and have everything you will need on hand.

Next, gather and prepare the equipment and ingredients. For cookie recipes, this may mean pre-heating the oven, greasing or lining a pan, and having all your wet and dry ingredients measured out in bowls or other containers beforehand, just as a recipe specifies. Some recipes will call for certain ingredients at different temperatures. For example, butter often needs to be at room temperature for easy creaming. Be aware that cold eggs fresh from the refrigerator are easier to separate, while those at room temperature are easier to whip up. Also make sure ingredients such as nuts or chocolate are chopped as directed.

QUALITY INGREDIENTS

Most cookies are made with a few relatively commonplace ingredients. For this reason, make sure that whatever you use is the freshest and the best quality. The difference will be apparent when you taste the finished cookies.

Try to buy flour in amounts that you expect to use within 4 to 6 months. It will keep longer than this, but it is best when fresh. Keep flour in an air-tight container, stored in a cool, dry place away from light.

Unsalted butter is best for baking cookies because it has a creamier, fresher taste. It also allows you to add salt to suit your taste. Purchase unsalted butter from markets with a high turnover to ensure freshness. It will keep in the refrigerator for about 3 weeks.

When purchasing eggs, look for large AA eggs. The grade "AA" refers to freshness and is the highest quality you can buy. Most cookie recipes are developed for large eggs, and using extra-large, jumbo, or small eggs will alter the results.

When using chocolate, purchase it from a store with good turnover. Premium brands, such as Callebaut, Scharffen Berger, and Valrhona, are available at some supermarkets and at specialty-food shops, and the better the chocolate you use, the better the cookie will taste. Always purchase the type specified in the recipe: semisweet (plain) or unsweetened chocolate. Semisweet and bittersweet are similar and can be used interchangeably. Store chocolate, well wrapped in foil or plastic, at cool room temperature.

Nuts and spices are also important cookie ingredients. For the best results, purchase nuts and spices from markets with good turnover. Nuts contain high amounts of oil and can turn rancid. Taste them before using to be certain they are fresh. If frozen in an airtight plastic container or heavy-duty freezer bag, nuts will keep for up to 1 year. Spices start to lose essential oils as soon as they are ground. Replace ground spices after 6 months and whole spices after 1 year. Buy spices in small amounts in bulk if possible, and label them with the date of purchase.

MEASURING

It is important to be accurate when measuring ingredients for making cookies. Every baker should have both dry and wet measuring cups. Dry measuring cups, which come as a nesting set, are usually made of stainless steel or plastic. Once you have filled the cup with the dry ingredient, use the dull side of a knife blade to level it off flush with the rim of the cup, to arrive at the exact amount. Liquid measuring cups look like pitchers and are usually made of clear glass or plastic. When measuring a liquid, place the cup on a flat surface, pour in the liquid, let it settle, and then read the measure at eye level.

Certain ingredients require extra care when measuring. Flour should be spooned into a measuring cup or at least stirred before scooping so as not to overpack the cup. Brown sugar, on the other hand, should be packed into a cup firmly enough that it retains the cup's shape when tapped out. Lightly rinsing a cup with cold water before pouring in a sticky ingredient such as molasses or honey will help it slip out easily.

Some recipes call for sifting flour or confectioners' (icing) sugar through a sifter or sieve, before or after it is measured, to aerate it. This will give the ingredient a uniform consistency, eliminating any clumps. Sifting will also increase volume, so do not sift before measuring unless a recipe specifies a sifted measurement.

ABOUT COOKIE DOUGH

Although cookie-making directions vary widely, every baker needs to master a few basic techniques that are common to many recipes. Keep in mind that nearly every cookie dough can be made by hand or machine.

CREAMING BUTTER AND SUGAR

Cookie recipes typically start with creaming the butter or creaming the butter with the sugar. To accomplish this, the butter is first beaten until it lightens in color, increases in volume, and is smooth and fluffy. This step will take 3 to 4 minutes with an electric mixer, or longer by hand. Do not rush this step; thorough creaming aerates the butter and contributes to a light texture.

Once the butter is creamed, add the sugar, again beating until the mixture is fluffy and light. At this point, the mixture becomes a batter and will be soft, smooth, and pale yellow or tan. The grains of sugar should be fully incorporated into the butter. If you rub a little creamed butter and sugar between your fingertips, the mixture should not feel gritty.

ADDING DRY INGREDIENTS

Sifting flour together with other dry ingredients such as baking powder and salt is the best way to combine and aerate these ingredients so that they distribute evenly and readily into a batter. Always add dry ingredients gradually and mix or stir just until they are no longer visible in the batter. Do not overmix; if the batter is overbeaten, the cookies will be tough.

DROP COOKIES

Shown opposite are the basic steps for making oatmeal, chocolate chip, or other drop cookies with an electric mixer.

1 **Creaming butter:** In a large bowl, cream the butter until fluffy and pale yellow. Add the sugar if specified in the recipe and continue to beat until the mixture no longer feels gritty when rubbed between your thumb and forefinger.

2 **Combining ingredients:** Add the flour mixture to the butter mixture gradually, mixing just until blended. At this point, add oats, nuts, chocolate chips, or other dried ingredients specified in a recipe.

3 **Forming drop cookies:** Scoop the batter by rounded tablespoons and use another spoon to push them off onto the prepared pans, spacing the cookies to allow for spreading.

4 **Transferring cookies:** Use a thin, flexible metal spatula to transfer the cookies while they are still warm to a wire rack to cool.

BAR COOKIES

Simple-to-make bar cookies, such as Brownies (page 29), result from soft, rich batters baked in straight-sided pans. As with a cake, use a toothpick or similar tool to ensure that the bars remain moist in the center. Once cooled, the sheet of bars is usually cut into squares or rectangles. Lining the pan with aluminum foil makes lifting out the finished bars easy.

ROLLED COOKIES

Most doughs for rolled cookies, such as Sugar Cookies (page 14), should be refrigerated for 30 minutes to 2 hours before rolling. On a lightly floured work surface, with a rolling pin, roll the chilled dough from the center toward the edge, using short strokes. Do not press down on the rolling pin so heavily that you crush the dough. While the dough is still thick, turn it over periodically or rotate it a quarter turn to prevent it from sticking. If cookie dough softens too much during rolling and becomes sticky, refrigerate it for 10 to 15 minutes, until firm enough to roll and cut.

The rolled-out dough should usually be ⅛ to ¼ inch (3 to 6 mm) thick. After cutting out as many cookies as you can from the initial rolling, gather any dough scraps together, reroll, and cut out additional cookies. Do not reroll dough scraps more than twice unless you are working with a very rich and buttery dough; if you do, your subsequent cookies may be tough. If cookie dough tears, repair it by pinching it back together.

REFRIGERATOR COOKIES

The dough for refrigerator cookies, also known as icebox cookies, is shaped into a log or block and chilled before slicing and baking. Different colors of dough can be used to make fun patterns in the final cookies. The dough can be made up to 2 days in advance, making refrigerator cookies especially convenient for the baker with a full schedule.

To form dough into logs, as for Neapolitan Cookies (page 46) or Pistachio-Spice Cookies (page 60), lay the dough down near the edge of a sheet of waxed paper or plastic wrap. Fold the paper or plastic over the dough and roll up tightly, forming a compact log or cylinder. Refrigerate for at least 2 hours, or preferably overnight, before cutting the dough into slices and baking.

PRESSED COOKIES

Using a cookie press, or cookie gun, is a simple way to make elegantly shaped cookies. The presses work best with fairly firm, pliable dough. For more information on using a cookie press, see the recipe for Spritz Cookies, page 76.

OVEN SAVVY

An accurate heat level is critical when baking cookies. Use an oven thermometer to determine your oven's accuracy. If the oven is off by 25° or 50°F (5° or 10°C), adjust the temperature dial accordingly. Most recipes are designed for baking on oven racks as close to the center of the oven as possible. If you are baking two sheets of cookies at a time and they will not both fit on one rack, place two racks as close to the center of the oven as possible.

If baking more than one sheet of cookies at a time, halfway through the baking time, switch the baking sheets between the racks and rotate them back to front. This will ensure more even browning.

COOLING

Cookie cooling instructions vary from recipe to recipe. Some cookies need to cool briefly or completely on the baking sheet, or in the case of bar cookies, in the baking pan, before being removed; others should be removed immediately. Follow the directions in the individual recipes.

It's a good idea to let baking sheets cool completely between batches. If you drop dough onto baking sheets still hot from the oven, the dough will begin to cook, softening and spreading, before you've dropped all the cookies. To save time, get each new batch of cookies ready on a piece of parchment (baking) paper, then slide it onto the baking sheet and slip the sheet immediately into the oven.

DECORATING

Allow enough time for cookies to cool completely before decorating them, and allow the decorations to set before serving. Handle decorated cookies with care to prevent cracking or disturbing the decorations. To store, wrap each cookie individually in a piece of plastic wrap or layer them loosely between sheets of waxed paper. Store in an airtight container.

DECORATING WITH ICING

A simple sugar cookie can be turned into a work of art with intricate designs and patterns made with icing. For detailed instructions on how to flow and pipe icing, see pages 92–96. If you want to use a variety of colors, be sure to have lots of small bowls on hand for mixing icing with different food colorings. Also have a pastry bag or two and tips ready for piping.

Set each pastry bag, fitted with its tip, in a small glass so it will stand upright while being filled. Some other tools to have on hand for icing are an offset spatula, a pastry brush, small spoons, and tweezers.

Practice piping designs onto a plate or a sheet of waxed paper. You can always scrape the icing from the plate and reuse it. If you are decorating on top of a solid layer of icing, be sure to let the first layer dry fully, usually 1 to 3 hours, before applying the new layer of icing.

COLORED SUGARS AND OTHER DECORATIONS

Today, a wide assortment of cookie decorations is available. You can find almost any shade of colored sugar, or you can even create your own shade with powdered food coloring. Sugars are also available in an assortment of grains, from fine to coarse, adding texture and sparkle to any cookie.

Some of the most traditional cookie decorations include raisins, dried cranberries, and chocolate sprinkles. Other ideas include shiny silver dragées, small pearlescent edible beads, and other small, hard candies.

To apply colored sugar or other decorations, spread baked cookies with a thin, even layer of Royal Icing (page 99). While the icing is still moist,

press the decorations down lightly with your fingertips to make sure they adhere. Tweezers assist in the most precise placement of decorations, and small spoons are helpful when you are applying colored sugars.

In general, cookies that are not iced must be decorated before they are baked. If the decorations are sticky (like cranberries, raisins, and other dried fruits), or if they are pieces of cookie dough, you can simply press the decorations into the dough. If the decorations are sugars, sprinkles, or candies, brush the baked cookie very lightly with beaten egg white (pages 113–14). Sprinkle on the decorations, pressing them down gently, and shake off any excess sugar or sprinkles.

CHOCOLATE

Use a chocolate coating to decorate or dip cookies. To make a chocolate coating, combine chopped chocolate with a little vegetable shortening (vegetable lard) in the top pan of a double boiler and melt over barely simmering water (page 50). The shortening is optional, but it helps to keep the chocolate looking shiny once it cools. Use 1 teaspoon vegetable shortening for every 4 oz (125 g) chocolate for best results.

To dip cookies in chocolate, hold the cookie firmly and dip it into the chocolate. Lift it out of the chocolate and set it on a rack over a tray or baking sheet lined with parchment paper. Let sit at room temperature or refrigerate until the chocolate is set, 30 minutes to 1 hour.

To drizzle cookies with chocolate, dip a teaspoon or a fork in warm chocolate and wave it back and forth over the cookies to create a series of thin, delicate lines. (See the recipe for Almond Crisps, page 50.)

STORING COOKIES

Most baked cookies and bars can be stored at room temperature for up to 3 days. Soft cookies with lots of fat, such as butter cookies or chocolate chip cookies, will not keep as long as crisper ones, such as biscotti. When fully cooled, cookies or cut bars should be transferred to an airtight container, such as a cookie tin or rigid plastic container. Bars that have not been cut and removed from the pan can be covered with foil and set aside at room temperature for up to a day.

Many cookie doughs can be frozen, particularly those designed for rolling into logs and slicing. Other good candidates include stiff, buttery doughs such as Sugar Cookies (page 14) or Spritz Cookies (page 76).

Most baked cookies and bars can be frozen for longer storage. Let them cool completely and then wrap in small stacks or individually in plastic wrap. Pack the wrapped cookies in rigid plastic containers or in zippered plastic freezer bags. Most cookies can be frozen for up to 3 months.

Thaw frozen cookies, still wrapped, at room temperature or in the refrigerator. Most will thaw within 2 hours. Serve them as soon as possible after they are fully thawed. They are not as moist as fresh-baked cookies and therefore tend to go stale faster.

Do not store crisp and cakey cookies together. The crisp cookies will absorb moisture from the others and soften. Store frosted or other decorated cookies in single layers, separated by waxed or parchment paper to prevent them from sticking together.

GIVING COOKIES

A gift of homemade cookies is always a welcome treat. When simply and creatively wrapped, a plate, box, or tin of cookies becomes the perfect gift, whether you are attending an open house or sending a care package.

If you are going to personally deliver the cookies, almost any recipe will work. If you are shipping the cookies, select fairly sturdy recipes, such as the ones in the Cookies for Giving chapter (page 59). Plastic wrap is a good way to protect cookies in transit. It insulates the cookies, keeps them fresh, and protects them if a package is handled roughly. Pack wrapped cookies snugly in a handsome tin or in a strong cardboard box. Set the tin or box inside a heavy-duty shipping container large enough to allow for the addition of packing materials. Tuck bubble wrap, tissue, or other cushioning material inside to keep the cookies from shifting. Tape the box securely, label it clearly, and ship it to arrive within a few days.

Shown opposite are some fun ideas for packaging cookies:

1 Packing in bags: Decorative bags are a quick way to package cookies, and they come in a wide variety of colors and sizes. If desired, use a length of pretty ribbon to add a festive touch.

2 Packing in boxes: Seek out cardboard boxes or sturdy paper take-out boxes with metal handles at craft stores. Arrange the cookies on a bed of shredded paper or tissue to prevent breakage.

3 Packing in tins: A traditional option for giving cookies, tins are perfect for stacking multiple layers. Look for tins with interesting shapes and textures.

4 Packing on a plate: Arrange cookies on an attractive plate or platter, then wrap in cellophane and tie with a length of ribbon. Include the recipe on a gift card if desired, so the recipient can make the cookies again.

GLOSSARY

BAKEWARE Different types of cookies require different types of bakeware. Below are some of the most common choices for making cookies.

Baking pan: Used for brownies or other bar cookies, baking pans can be deep glass or ceramic dishes or metal pans. They come in all shapes and sizes. Foods bake more quickly in glass and ceramic dishes, so if a recipe has been written for a metal pan, you may need to reduce baking times and temperatures if using a baking dish.

Baking sheet: The most commonly used pan for baking cookies, a baking sheet is a rectangular metal pan with shallow, slightly sloping rims. It comes in several forms, including the half-sheet pan and the jelly-roll pan.

Cookie sheet: Flat metal pans, cookie sheets usually have a low rim on one or two ends to allow for sliding cookies onto a cooling rack. Avoid very dark sheets, which may cause your cookies to over-brown or burn. Nonstick cookie sheets work well and are easy to clean. Insulated cookie sheets, which have an interior air pocket between two layers of metal, guarantee that no cookie will ever have an overbrowned bottom. They do not, however, work well for thin, crisp cookies, which benefit from intense heat. You will want to have at least 2 cookie sheets on hand when baking big batches of cookies.

BAKING POWDER VS. BAKING SODA Baking powder and baking soda are chemical leaveners. They work by reacting with both liquids and heat to release carbon dioxide gas, which in turn leavens a batter, causing it to rise as it cooks. Baking powder is a mixture of an acid and an alkaline, or base, that is activated when it is exposed to moisture or heat. Double-acting baking powder contains two acids. The first acid reacts while mixing the batter, and the second acid reacts in the oven during the baking process.

Baking soda, also called bicarbonate of soda, is an alkaline, or base, that releases carbon dioxide gas only when it comes into contact with an acidic ingredient, such as sour cream, butter-milk, or molasses.

BUTTERSCOTCH The term *butterscotch* refers to the flavor that develops when butter, brown sugar, and a little vanilla are blended together.

BUTTER, UNSALTED Also called sweet butter, unsalted butter is favored for baking. It lacks the addition of salt that can interfere with the taste of the final recipe and is likely to be fresher since salt acts as a preservative.

CHOCOLATE See pages 29 and 105.

COCOA POWDER See page 38.

COOKIE CUTTERS Some cookie cutters are made of plastic, but the best cutters are made of metal, so that the cutting side holds its edge. Cookie cutters come in different shapes and sizes, from basic rounds to holiday icons and seasonal motifs. When using cookie cutters, dip them in flour periodically so they won't stick to the dough and cut as many cookies as you can at one time. Carefully lift away the unshaped edges (scraps), and use a wide spatula to transfer the cutout cookies to the prepared baking sheet.

COOLING RACKS Cookies just out of the oven, either removed with a spatula or still on the pan, are cooled on wire racks, which permit air to circulate on all sides. The racks, which come in squares, rectangles, and rounds and stand on short legs, are made of tinned steel, stainless steel, anodized aluminum, or chrome- or nickel-plated metal. Have on hand enough racks to handle 2 baking sheets of cookies.

CREAM OF TARTAR This white powder is potassium tartrate, a by-product of wine making. It is primarily used in baking to stabilize egg whites so that they whip up more easily.

EGG, RAW Eggs are sometimes used raw in icing, as a sticky base for sugar or other decorations, and other cookie preparations. Raw eggs run a risk of being infected with salmonella or other bacteria, which can lead to food poisoning. This risk is of most concern to small children, older people, pregnant women, and anyone with a compromised immune system. If you have health and safety concerns, do not consume raw egg. You can substitute raw eggs in some recipes with pasteurized egg products such as meringue powder.

EXTRACTS Concentrated flavorings made from plants, extracts, also called essences, are often used to flavor sweet recipes. Extracts are made by distilling the essential oils of a plant and then suspending the oils in alcohol. Among the most common extracts used in cookie baking are vanilla, almond, anise, and mint. Avoid imitation flavorings, which rely on synthetic compounds and have a less complex flavor. Store extracts in a cool, dark place for up to 1 year.

FLOUR
All-Purpose: Also known as plain flour, all-purpose flour is the popular general-use flour that is good for a wide range of cookies and other desserts. It is made from a mixture of soft and hard wheats.

Cake: Low in protein and high in starch, cake flour is milled from soft wheat and contains cornstarch. It is very fine in texture and has also undergone a bleaching process that increases its ability to hold water and sugar. Cookies made with cake flour have a particularly tender crumb.

FLOUR SIFTER Shaped like a canister, and activated by a handle that is turned or squeezed, a flour sifter forces flour, confectioners' (icing) sugar, or other ingredients through a layer (or two or three) of wire mesh. A fine-mesh sieve may be used instead by simply tapping its rim to pass the flour through.

MERINGUE POWDER This pasteurized egg product, made from egg whites, sugar, cornstarch (cornflour), vanilla flavoring, and other ingredients, allows bakers to avoid the use of raw egg whites, which in rare instances can be a health risk. Once opened, store in an airtight container in the refrigerator.

MOLASSES See page 80.

NUTS
Below are some nuts commonly used in cookie recipes. For information on toasting nuts, see page 22, and for grinding nuts, see page 37.

Almonds: These oval nuts are the meat found inside the pit of a dried fruit related to the peach. Almonds are delicate and fragrant and have a smooth texture. They are sold unblanched, with their natural brown skins intact, and blanched, with the skins removed to reveal their light ivory color.

Brazil nuts: Enclosed in a dark, hard, roughly textured shell shaped like a small orange segment, Brazil nuts taste somewhat like the meat of a coconut. The seeds of very tall trees that grow only in tropical regions of South America, they require time and skill to harvest. Brazil nuts are best eaten as snacks or used in desserts.

Hazelnuts: Also known as filberts, grape-sized hazelnuts have hard shells that come to a point like an acorn, cream-colored flesh, and a sweet, rich, buttery flavor. Difficult to crack, they are usually sold already shelled.

Macadamia nuts: See page 72.

Pecans: See page 84.

Pistachios: Pistachios have creamy tan, thin, hard, rounded outer shells. As the nuts ripen, their shells crack to reveal light green kernels.

Walnuts: The furrowed, double-lobed nutmeat of the walnut has an assertive, rich flavor. The most common variety is the English walnut, also known as Persian walnut, which has a light brown shell that cracks easily. Black walnuts have a stronger flavor and extremely hard shells but are a challenge to find.

PARCHMENT PAPER Treated to withstand the high heat of an oven, parchment paper is ideal for lining pans for baking cookies. Also known as baking paper, parchment resists moisture and grease and has a smooth surface that prevents cookies from sticking. Look for parchment paper in well-stocked markets and cookware shops.

SPATULAS Cookie bakers regularly use both metal and rubber spatulas. The offset spatula has a thin, flexible blade, usually of stainless steel, that rises in an angle off of the handle. These spatulas are ideal for removing delicate cookies from baking sheets. Wide, flat, thin metal spatulas, also known as turners, can also be used for lifting cookies from pans. Flexible rubber spatulas, available in varying sizes, are excellent for stirring or folding in ingredients and for scraping down bowl or food processor sides.

SPICES

Below are some spices used in making many cookies. For information on using spices, see page 79.

Allspice: See page 71.

Aniseed: See page 18.

Cinnamon: The dark bark of a tree, the most commonly found variety is cassia cinnamon, which is a dark red-brown and has a strong, sweet taste. Cinnamon is available in stick form or already ground. If you grind your own cinnamon, first break or crush the stick into pieces.

Cloves: Shaped like a small nail with a round head, the almost-black clove is the dried bud of a tropical evergreen tree. It has a strong, sweet flavor with a peppery quality and is available whole or ground.

Ginger: A knobby, brown rhizome, or underground stem, from a tropical plant, ginger has a warm, spicy fragrance and flavor. For cookies and other baked goods, ginger is most often used ground or in pieces that have been crystallized,

or candied. You can find crystallized ginger in specialty-food shops or the baking or Asian food section of well-stocked grocery stores.

Nutmeg: See page 46.

SUGAR

Brown: See page 30.

Coarse crystals: Also called coarse sugar or sanding sugar, this decorative sugar is appreciated for its large, pretty granules.

Colored: See page 95.

Confectioners': Also called powdered or icing sugar, confectioners' sugar is granulated sugar that has been crushed to a powder and mixed with a little cornstarch (cornflour).

Granulated: The most common sugar is granulated white sugar, which has been extracted from sugarcane or beets and refined by boiling, centrifuging, chemical treatment, and straining. For baking, buy only sugar labeled cane sugar; beet sugar may have an unpredictable effect on many recipes.

Maple: Made from boiling maple sap almost dry, maple sugar is twice as sweet as granulated white sugar.

Raw: Most sugars marketed as "raw" are actually partially refined. Turbinado, a common raw sugar, has light brown, coarse crystals. Demerara and Barbados are also varieties of raw sugar.

Superfine: When finely ground, granulated sugar becomes superfine sugar, also

known as caster sugar. Because it dissolves rapidly, it is preferred for delicate mixtures such as beaten egg whites. To make your own, process granulated sugar in a food processor until finer granules form.

VANILLA EXTRACT Also known as vanilla essence, this distillation lends perfume, depth, and nuance to cookies. Avoid imitation vanilla, which is artificially flavored and has an inferior taste. Vanilla extract is most commonly made from Bourbon-Madagascar beans, and the best-quality vanilla extracts should state this on their label.

ZEST The zest is the thin, colored portion of a citrus rind. Choose organic fruit for any recipe calling for zest, then be sure to scrub the fruit well to eliminate any residue or wax. You can use a zester, a tool designed for removing the zest in long, narrow strips, which can then be left whole or chopped. Or, use a fine Microplane grater or the finest rasps of a handheld grater-shredder. In every case, take care to remove only the colored portion of the rind, leaving behind all of the bitter white pith.

INDEX

SIMON & SCHUSTER SOURCE
A Division of Simon & Schuster, Inc.
Rockefeller Center
1230 Avenue of the Americas
New York, NY 10020

WILLIAMS-SONOMA
Founder and Vice-Chairman: Chuck Williams
Book Buyer: Cecilia Prentice

WELDON OWEN INC.
Chief Executive Officer: John Owen
President: Terry Newell
Chief Operating Officer: Larry Partington
Vice President, International Sales: Stuart Laurence
Creative Director: Gaye Allen
Series Editor: Sarah Putman Clegg
Associate Editor: Heather Belt
Art Director: Catherine Jacobes
Designer: Teri Gardiner
Production Manager: Chris Hemesath
Shipping and Production Coordinator: Libby Temple

Weldon Owen wishes to thank the following
people for their generous assistance and
support in producing this book: Copy Editor
Carolyn Miller; Consulting Editor Sharon Silva;
Designer Douglas Chalk; Stylist George Dolese;
Cover Food Stylists Kim Konecny and Erin Quon;
Associate Food Stylist and Recipe Consultant
Elisabet der Nederlanden; Recipe Consultant
Peggy Fallon; Decorating Consultant Diane Gsell;
Photographer's Assistants Noriko Akiyama and
Heidi Ladendorf; Proofreaders Desne Ahlers and
Carrie Bradley; and Indexer Ken DellaPenta.

Williams-Sonoma Collection *Cookies* was
conceived and produced by Weldon Owen Inc.,
814 Montgomery Street, San Francisco,
California 94133, in collaboration with
Williams-Sonoma, 3250 Van Ness Avenue,
San Francisco, California 94109

A Weldon Owen Production
Copyright © 2002 by Weldon Owen Inc. and
Williams-Sonoma Inc.

For information about special discounts for
bulk purchases, please contact Simon & Schuster
Special Sales: 1-800-456-6798 or
business@simonandschuster.com

Set in Trajan, Utopia, and Vectora.

Color separations by Bright Arts Graphics
Singapore (Pte.) Ltd.
Printed and bound in Singapore by Tien Wah
Press (Pte.) Ltd.

First printed in 2002.

10 9 8 7 6 5 4 3 2 1

Library of Congress Cataloging-in-Publication
Data is available.

ISBN 0-7432-2683-6

A NOTE ON WEIGHTS AND MEASURES

All recipes include customary U.S. and metric measurements. Metric conversions are based on
a standard developed for these books and have been rounded off. Actual weights may vary.